AGRICULTURAL FINANCE IN JAMMU & KASHMIR

AGRICULTURAL FINANCE IN JAMMU & KASHMIR

By

JARNAIL SINGH MALHOTRA

ANMOL PUBLICATIONS PVT. LTD.
NEW DELHI-110 002 (INDIA)

ANMOL PUBLICATIONS PVT. LTD.
4374/4B, Ansari Road, Daryaganj
New Delhi-110 002

Agricultural Finance in Jammu & Kashmir

First Edition 1998
ISBN 81-261-0034-6

PRINTED IN INDIA

Published by J.L. Kumar for Anmol Publications Pvt. Ltd., New Delhi-110 002 and Printed at Mehra Offset Press, Delhi.

CONTENTS

Preface		*vii*
Acknowledgement		*ix*
Chapter-1:	**Introduction**	1
	- The Necessity of Agricultural Finance - Nature and Objectives of the Study - Hypotheses - Methodology - Research Design - Scope	
Chapter-2:	**Agriculture Situation in Jammu and Kashmir**	16
	- Land Use pattern - Cropping Pattern - Land Holdings - Irrigation - New Agricultural Strategy - Implements and Machinery - Position of Agriculture in State's Economy - Position of Agricultural Finance in the State	
Chapter-3:	**Socio-economic Characteristics of People in Jammu Division**	23
	- Sex and Age Composition - Family Size and Availability of Land per Capita - Educational Status	

- Distribution of Land Holdings
- Extent of Tenancy
- Land Use Pattern
- Economic Status of the Population
- Farm Family Assets
- Family Income

Chapter-4: Sources of Finance 74

- Distribution of Finance according to Sources
- Distribution of Finance by Commercial Banks in Jammu Division
- Distribution of Agricultural Finance by Regional Rural Banks
- Distribution of Agricultural Finance by Central Co-operative Land Dev. Banks
- Distribution of Agricultural Finance by Co-operative Banks and Societies
- Source-wise Distribution of Agricultural Finance to Different Groups of Farmers
- Block-wise Distribution of Agricultural Finance according to Sources and Beneficiaries
- Purpose-wise Distribution of Finance to Different Size Groups
- Source of Finance according to Purposes
- Extent of Outstandings in Jammu Division
- Trend of Outstandings in Jammu Division

Chapter-5 : Problems of Agricultural Finance 126

- Problems faced by the Agriculturists
- Problems faced by the Institutions

Chapter-6 : Conclusion and Suggestions 138

- Conclusion
- Suggestions

Appendices 150

Bibliography 162

PREFACE

Finance is the most important lubricant in every production activity whether agriculture or industry. An average agriculturist is a poor man, with very limited means at his disposal. He does not have much savings to fall back upon. For every extraordinary need which falls outside his routine livelihood, he needs credit/finance facilities. These needs possess wide spectrum from performing social ceremonies to purchase of seeds, fertilizers and agricultural implements.

It is true, for stimulating the tempo of agricultural production, it is necessary that farmers must be provided with adequate and timely finance for fertilizers, improved seeds, modern implements, etc. The nationalisation of the 14 major commercial banks in July 1969, and the establishment of five Regional Rural Banks on 2nd October 1975, marked the beginning of a determined effort to promote development of agriculture through the network of banking system. But it is unfortunate that agricultural finance is still a problem; it has not been solved, though commercial banks are the major sources of agricultural finance.

In this context, the present research project makes an indepth study of agricultural finance relating to institutional sources. It seeks to examine in detail their role in providing agricultural finance, problems faced by the agriculturists in obtaining finance and likewise the problems faced by the institutions in providing finance. In the light of problems faced by the beneficiaries and the institutions suitable measures have been suggested to overcome these problems.

The methodology of the present study is based on field survey conducted by the researcher personally of 40 villages selected at random from four blocks — two each in Jammu and Poonch districts of Jammu Division. In all, 200 houses were selected at random at the rate of five households from each village. Similarly bank branches operating in the area covered under study were taken for detailed study. In addition, for this purpose two set of questionnaires were designed, which were personally filled in by the researcher by contacting on spot the beneficiaries and the bank branches. Published and unpublished data available in books, journals, reports etc. was also utilised to complete the study.

This study is divided into six chapters. The necessity and sources for agricultural financing, nature and objectives of the study, hypothesis, methodology and research design and the scope of the study have been presented in the first chapter.

In the second chapter we have analysed the rural economy of Jammu and Kashmir state; land-use pattern, cropping pattern, irrigation, land-holdings, new agricultural strategy and the position of agriculture in State's economy.

The third chapter discusses the Socio-economic Characteristics of the sample beneficiaries like distribution of population by sex and age, average family size, educational status of the population, size of holdings, extent of tenancy, types of land-holdings, economic status of the population, farm family assets and family incomes.

In the fourth chapter, an attempt is made to analyse the extent of agriculture finance provided by all financial institutions existed in the area covered under survey and the purpose-wise distribution of finance by different institutions to different groups of borrowers.

The fifth chapter consists of the problems faced by the agriculturists and the institutions which cause hindrance for the effective growth of agricultural operations.

The sixth and the last chapter consists of conclusion and suggestions to overcome the problems faced by the agriculturists and the institutions.

The study may prove beneficial to the Government, the Reserve Bank of India, the Commercial Banks, researchers and all beneficiaries.

Jarnail Singh Malhotra

ACKNOWLEDGEMENTS

I express my deepest sense of gratitude and indebtedness to Prof. N.S. Gupta, Professor of Financial Management, Institute of Management and Public Administration, J&K Govt., for his able guidance, keen interest, constant encouragement, untiring and ever-willing help during the entire period of this study.

I am profoundly indebted to Dr. S.P. Gupta, Reader, P.G. Department of Commerce, University of Jammu, for taking personal interest in completing my work. I have been benefitted by his constructive criticisms and analytical suggestions.

My sincere thanks are due to Prof. P.N. Abrol, Head, P.G. Department of Commerce, University of Jammu, Dr. R.D. Sharma, Reader, Department of Commerce, University of Jammu for their constant encouraging attitude towards me.

I am thankful to the authorities of the Punjab National Bank, Rural Banks, State Bank of India and Co-operative Societies for their help in the research. My sincere thanks are also due to the villagers whom I administered the questionnaires.

I am also grateful to Dr. Anil Gupta, Dr. Amrik Singh and Mr. Manohar Lal Gupta for their encouragement in the completion of this research work.

I am highly thankful to Mr. Mangal Singh, U.D.C., Sanskrit Vidyapeeth, Jammu for typing this manuscript carefully.

My deepest sense of gratitudes are due to my parents, brother, wife and sweet children for their constant encouragement.

Jarnail Singh Malhotra

1
INTRODUCTION

Agriculture is the core sector of Indian economy; it accounts for about 34.8 per cent of the national income and provides livelihood to about 66.7 per cent of the working population of the country. It has also been the source of raw materials to our leading industries such as sugar, cotton and jute, textiles, hydrogenated oils, food products, soap and other agro-based industries which together account for 50 per cent of income generated in the manufacturing sector of India.

Agriculture products like tea, sugar, oil-seeds, tobacco, spices, etc. constitute the main items of export of India. Roughly speaking the proportion of agricultural goods which are exported may account for 50 per cent of our exports and the manufacture with agricultural content (such goods as manufactured jute cloth and sugar) contribute another 20 per cent or so this making 70 per cent of India's exports.

In India, there are about 30 crores cattle. The fodder is provided by agriculture to them. Cattle is also a form of wealth in India.

Transport agencies secure most of their business from the movement of agricultural goods. Foodgrains, raw materials and other agricultural products are transported in bulk from the producing regions to the consuming regions. Their movement helps sustain the vast network of roads and railways, etc. It is true to say that both agriculture and transport act as complementary to each other.

In short, it has been rightly observed that agriculture is the backbone of the Indian economy. No scheme or programme of economic development and welfare can afford to ignore this reality of the Indian economic situation. It is way the importance of agriculture, despite rapid industrialisation has not in any way diminished. In the wake of growing commitments of the government to realize the goals of self-reliance and welfare state, it has become necessary not to achieve self-sufficiency in food and agricultural raw materials, but also to modernise agriculture.

R.L. Cohen, justly remarks, "In the global context food, a prime necessity of life, is an agricultural product, and the world still needs to devote a part of its resources to the production of necessities.[1] In view of its vital role in providing food and fibre for the ever increasing population besides direct employment to about 40 per cent of the world populace, it has become a tool for international politics, at least in the hands of so-called developed nation. Indeed, the study of the metamorphosis of the agriculture, from a mere primitive occupation to eke out living to its highly sophisticated stage of development, is extremely fascinating.

Agriculture, like industry requires capital. A close examination of agricultural development showed that the target of foodgrain has touched a new height of 176.4 million tonnes in 1990-91 as against 150 million tonnes achieved in 1984-85. For stimulating the tempo of agricultural production, it is necessary that farmer must be provided with adequate and timely finance for fertilizers, improved seeds, modern implements, etc. In this context, the present research takes up this universal phenomenon of agricultural credit and its necessity in terms of the financial provisions and its channelisation in agricultural areas of the different parts of the state. For without proper and sufficient financial investment in the agricultural field, there is no possibility to modernise it and raised it to the optimum level and meet the growing and changing standards of life. One of the basic needs for augmenting agricultural production is the credit requirement of the Indian farmers. On the provision of adequate credit, agricultural self-sufficiency would be assumed. Therefore, there is a need for agricultural finance.

The Necessity for Agricultural Finance

One of the basic needs of augmenting agricultural production is the credit requirement of the Indian farmers. If we can provide adequate credit to the Indian farmers, agricultural self-sufficiency would be ensured. It is very significant to notice that the intelligentsia of our country has realised the importance of agriculture and the crucial role it plays in the Indian economy.

Agricultural finance is of crucial importance to a farmer. Modern agricultural development require heavy investment in current inputs like high-yielding variety seeds, fertilizers and pesticides and modern technology in the form of machinery and equipment and other infrastructural facilities like irrigation and land development etc. The vast majority of Indian farmers has no savings for investment purposes and would be deprived of the benefits of modern technology if finance is not available to them to buy various inputs.

The concern of the present study, however, is to show that financial benefits to the farmers, can be rendered potentially viable, if there is support in terms of irrigation facilities, supplies of inputs, services such as tractor ploughing, technical guidance and so on. However, to begin with credit is inevitable and it has scope to advance any programme. Credit is an essential aspect of form operation particularly in case of small farmers. But in our state it is shy and not adequately available. Credit that is available in the market goes to the more powerful farm operators. The small farmer's share is maximum because of their potentiality in size, so in terms of maximisation of social welfare, they deserved a significant portion of national income. F.A. Nicholson's Report regarding the possibility of introducing Land and Agricultural Banks into the Madras Presidency, observes then as "essential of agriculture is credit". When credit is so essential, it is important to study its meaning, nature and character, sources for providing it and the basic issues and problems connected with it.

To speak more precisely, credit is the heart of the agrarian system in India. The credit needs of the farmers in relation to the requirements of their land and the quality of the production is classified into three categories:

1. **Short-term loans:** are required for purchase of the livestock, marketing of agricultural produce, payment of wages to hired labour, buying of seeds, fertilisers, fodder for cattle etc. The period of such loans is less than 15 months and generally granted by money-lenders and co-operative societies. Such loans are to be repaid after the harvest.

2. **Medium-term loans:** are received for the purchase of cattle, small agricultural implements, pump sets, electric motors, power tillers, threshers, for repair and construction of wells and for the reclamation of land, etc. The period of such loans ranges

from 2 years to 5 years.[2] These loans are generally provided by money-lenders, relatives of the farmers, co-operative societies and commercial banks.

3. **Long-term loans:** are required for effecting permanent improvement on land, digging tubewells, purchase of large agricultural implements and machinery like heavy tractors, harvesters, etc. and repayment of old debts. The period of such loans is extended beyond 5 years. Such loans are normally taken from land development banks.

In addition to these land-based schemes, the commercial banks also offer loans for the formation of certain allied activities like dairy farming and poultry farming, etc.

The extent of financial assistance would generally be restricted to seventy five per cent of the expected expenditure, in case of crop loans. The scales are fixed on the basis of the survey conducted by the banks themselves or on the basis of those arrived by the co-operative societies. The tangible security for a crop loan is the standing crop itself.

The new agricultural strategy has given birth to multiple cropping; that has kept the farmers busily engaged in their fields. Proper agriculture finance, will not only help multiple cropping but also provide diverse employment opportunities. It will increase the income of farmers, resulting in their less need of loan for consumption purposes like meeting of their immediate and day-to-day needs during the off-season.

The different sources that provide credit and finance facilities to the farmers are:

(i) Indigenous bankers or local merchants called Sahukar or Seth.

(ii) Merchants and commission agents,

(iii) Landlords,

(iv) Co-operative Societies,

(v) Land Mortgage or Land Development Banks,

(vi) Commercial Banks,

(vii) State Bank of India and the Reserve Bank of India,

(viii) NABARD (National Bank for Agriculture and Rural Development), and

(ix) Regional Rural Banks.

In order to stop the malpractices of the moneylenders, who indulge in all sorts of tricks to misled and cheat the farmers, the efforts were made to evolve a cooperative system of credit facilities. The Banking Commission reviewed the working of Cooperative Credit Organisations, particularly at grass root level and made a number of important recommendations in that behalf. While the cooperative banks had the necessary structure and their roots in the rural areas coupled with knowledge of local conditions and problems, they lacked in adequate resources and higher standard of management policy.

In view of the above observation, it was recommended that commercial and cooperative banks, must come closer together in meeting the credit needs of the farmers. There is need of replacement of the existing weak societies by rural cooperative banks or rural subsidiary banks. The form of organisation must essentially be co-operative and rural-based. However, technical and financial assistance in adequate measure was contemplated to flow either from district central co-operative bank or a commerical bank.

The thinking has gained further momentum particularly when commercial banks have been permitted to provide all types of credit to the farmers. The question is whether cooperative credit system should also be asked to emulate the examples of commercial banks and reshape their credit policy and operations accordingly. The functioning of the rural branches of the commercial banks has revealed that they have succeeded in mobilising huge amount of deposits from the rural areas but as far as their lending operations and other services are concerned, they have not been commensurate with the deposits mobilised and large sections of the needy people have remained out of their pail. The movement of nationalisation has widened the banking activity in rural areas. Between July 1969 and April 1990, about 62 per cent of new branches, opened by the nationalised commercial banks have been set up in the rural areas.

In the meantime, the new strategy for agricultural development necessitated the provision of heavy investment credit and production finance at a faster rate. The 14 big commercial banks were nationalised and inducted into the field of agricultural finance. The nationalised commercial banks were directed to undertake fast expansion of rural branches and provide direct and indirect finance to the priority sector of agriculture and rural industries. Thus, the institutional system of agricultural finance came to be constituted of the cooperatives on the one hand and the commercial banks on the other.

After about 5 years of bank nationalisation, it was realised that the commercial banks were also not in a position to meet the challenge and take credit and banking facilities to the door-steps of every rural entrepreneur. They not only suffered from the organisational gaps and personal deficiencies, but their methods and operations could not be changed to suit the objectives of rural credit.

Thus the latest invention in this field came to be the establishment of 5 regional rural banks started on 2nd October 1975 to cover the neglected areas and weaker sections of the people; as at the beginning of the eighth plan on April 1, 1990, 196 such branches have been set up in different areas of the country. It is estimated that 75% of the total financial needs of the Indian agriculturists are now being met by the institutional agencies like the commercial banks, regional rural banks and the co-operative societies.

The target of Co-operative Societies for the year 1989-90 was Rs.5540 crores for short-term loans and Rs.1530 crores for medium and long-term loans. As against this, short-term loans by Co-operative societies stood at Rs.4133.3 crores in 1989-90 while medium and long-term loans stood at Rs.1436.8 crores. Loans issued by Land Development Banks for long-term in 1989-90 were Rs.774 crores as against the target of Rs.1030 crores.

The advances from public sector banks to agriculture have grown to Rs.15082 crores as against the target of Rs.14585 crores for the year 1989-90.

The total quantum of agricultural credit disbursed by the institutional agencies has been increasing over the years. Total agricultural credit disbursed during 1985-86 was of the order of Rs.7354 crores which increased to Rs.7602 crores during 1986-87, Rs.8214 crores during 1987-88, Rs.11751 crores during 1988-89 and further to Rs.15082 crores during 1989-90.

What is needed now is quality and an all-out effort to bridge the yawning gap between credit demand and supply that will become evident in the coming years.[3] As shown in Table 1.1 the direct demand for agricultural credit will gradually rise from Rs.27,551 crores in 1989-90 to Rs.57317 crores in 1994-95 and further to Rs.1,10,873 crores in 1999-2000. As against this, the resources available in the banking system would be of the order of Rs.28,694 crores, Rs.51,829 crores and Rs.89,447 crores respectively. Serious efforts will have to be made to cover up the projected deficit of Rs.5487 crores in 1984-95 and Rs.21,426 crores in 1999-2000.

Table 1.1

Projected Demand and Supply for Rural Credit

(Rs. in Crores)

	1989-90	*1994-95*	*1999-2000*
Demand	27,551	57,316	1,10,873
Supply	28,694	51,829	89,447
Surplus (+)	+ 1,143	—	—
Deficit (–)	—	- 5,487	– 21,426

Source: M.L. Dantwala, op. cit., Table 2, p. 7.

The decision of the government to write off the loans upto Rs.10,000 of small, marginal and landless cultivators and artisans, as on October 2, 1989 has created a new set of problems. On the economic front, this measure will imply a total burden of more than Rs.8000 crores on the central and state governments, worsening the fiscal imbalance in the economy.[1] On the political front, this measure may give a wrong signal the rural borrowers and they might treat institutional credit at par with grants of subsidies provided by the government. As noted by ACRC (Agricultural Credit Review Committee), apart from the fact that measures such as write-off place heavy burden on the state exchequer, "they generate a general psychology of non-repayment, totally vitiating the recovery climate which, in the long-run, jeopardises the financial interests of the credit agencies."

The purpose of finance must enable the farmers to plan his cropping in the best possible way, recognising the cost of production of each crop well in advance of each sowing. Co-operative banks and commercial banks should advance adequate and timely loans to farmers. Moreover, "inadequate and delayed loans are worse than not financing them at all."

Basically in utilizing the loans in best possible manner, the farmers need to be educated in production and marketing of crops. They should be made to acquire the knowledge about modes of modern technology, marketing of crops, purchase of machinery etc. The banks must not make their "procedure of borrowing" very "cumbersome" and provide also assistance to farmers by their field staff and exports. In the remote villages of the state, there is a great need of opening rural branches of commercial banks and the Reserve Bank should "gear up its machinery so that there is no procedural delay."[5]

Nature and Objectives of the Thesis

Background

It is truism to say that agriculture forms the "Core Sector" of the Indian economy, that provides livelihood for more than sixty five per cent of the working population of the country. But, unfortunately, with all the modern technology and the financial resources for the agriculture sector, it is difficult to say with any certainty, that the problems of agriculture and finance, have been adequately solved or that it is nearing solution. This needs more time, patience and thought to penetrate more deeper into the problem and touch the roots to find out reasonable solution. Unfortunately in our state, the response and interest of the rural people to new technology and the renovated methods of farming is low and poor, because of his illiteracy and lack of financial resources. They need to be equipped with better financial resources, only then they shall be able to derive benefits of new technology.

There is no doubt, that a multi-agency approach of the government has assigned the responsibility of farm development to co-operatives, commercial banks and regional rural banks; but the farmers in villages are still illiterate, sunk in poverty, with their brood of children, they are yet sleeping on the thorns of heavy debts. These agencies have, at best routed out the non-institutional (especially the agricultural money-lenders) agents from the scene; but not yet removed the poverty of the farmers and brought peace, prosperity and security to the villages.

The study propose to observe that the services rendered by the cooperatives are not free from certain "imbalances". The studies on cooperative credit indicate that the benefits have gone to those who could manipulate things for themselves and for the favourite few. Not much of it has flown to backward areas of the states. Even the commercial banks "do not have the organisation or the expertise to deal with a vast number of cultivators spread over innumerable small villages." Moreover, the non-official leadership representing the cooperatives is found generally opposed to entry of the banks into this sphere.

At the time of nationalisation, the commercial banks were given special directive for more emphasis to the hitherto neglected and economically weaker section. It was to ensure that bank finances are made available to the productive needs of all sectors of the population, irrespective of the size and social status of a beneficiary. But, this has not yet found a practical footing, as, the villagers are yet fighting for their caste loyalties. There is still a great need to finance small and potentially viable farmers, as an experiment in "productive and incremental income oriented lending", based on the viability of a project rather than to the credit worthyness of the borrower, in the traditional sense.

The study propose to provide a substantive basis to examine the extent to which these objectives have been met. A closer examination shall reveal that the zeal with which these banks had entered the agricultural field has been ebbed down and slackned. There exists uneven and irrational distribution of credit between states and between regions within a state. In fact, the credit activity is confined to "selected-pockets", and the quantum of credit flown to the areas wherein the concentration of small holdings is high, is weak and indeed paltry. There is a break down of advance and it reveals an inverse relationship between the holding size and the number of borrowal accounts. Hence, the problem of agricultural finance with its two inter-related aspects of agriculturists and institutions providing agriculture finance has been chosen for the study.

Objects of the Study

The main objects of this study are:

1. To identify the sources of agricultural finance;
2. To examine the role of institutional agencies in providing finance for agricultural operations;
3. To study problems faced by the agriculturists and the institutions; and
4. To suggest suitable measures to overcome the problems faced by the agriculturists and the institutions.

Hypothesis

The hypothesis for the study are:

1. Commercial banks are the major source of agricultural finance in Jammu Division.
2. Agriculture Finance is endowed with a number of problems which affects the beneficiaries as well as the institutions.

Methodology

The research methodology adopted for the present investigation can be classified under two heads:

1. Direct investigation method based on field survey of 40 villages selected from Jammu Division; and
2. Reliance on the published and unpublished data obtained from publications and reports.

Research Design

The present study relates to Jammu Division of Jammu and Kashmir State. Jammu Division has six districts. Out of these six districts, District Jammu and District Poonch are selected. The former is much developed and the latter is comparatively under-developed. Both the districts — Jammu and Poonch have 5 and 3 tehsils respectively. Out of these 8 tehsils, Tehsil Ranbir Singh Pura and Tehsil Jammu have been selected from Jammu District and Tehsil Haveli and Tehsil Mender from Poonch District for study. The scope of the study is further restricted to selected villages of four blocks. The selected blocks are R.S. Pura from R.S. Pura Tehsil, Dansal from Jammu Tehsil, Haveli from Haveli Tehsil and Mendhar from Mendhar Tehsil. Out of these four blocks one each is developed and the other is under-developed in both Jammu and Poonch districts.

Selection of Villages

The selection of villages for observation and for the collection of data has been done on the basis of the developed and under-developed places. In all forty villages, ten each from R.S. Pura block, Dansal block, Haveli block and Mendhar block were selected at random for the study purpose. R.S. Pura block and Haveli block are developed and the other two Dansal block and Mendhar block are under-developed. The list of the selected villages is given on the next page.

R.S. Pura Block:

1. Raipur Gujran
2. Dabler
3. Baispur
4. Pralah
5. Chakroi
6. Pholora
7. Suchet Garh
8. Chuhala
9. Jindler
10. Paryal Bhrahmana

Dansal Block:

1. Smral
2. Shurta
3. Sandrote
4. Manwal
5. Ban
6. Chak Rakhwalian
7. Dokh Waziran
8. Khanpur
9. Jagti
10. Kameeni

Haveli Block:

1. Kunian

2. Khanetar
3. Shapur
4. Bandi Chachian
5. Dalan
6. Degwar Terwan
7. Gulpar
8. Karmara
9. Chandok
10. Timrah

Mendhar Block:

1. Harni
2. Ari
3. Salwah
4. Banala
5. Golutta
6. Jugal
7. Golad
8. Kasbalari
9. Sagra
10. Goi.

Selection of Farmers

It was decided to draw a sample of five households from each of the 40 villages of R.S. Pura, Dansal, Haveli and Mendhar blocks covered under study. In this way 200 households/farmers (50 from each block) were selected at random from these four blocks.

Collection of Data

In order to meet the demands of study and fulfil the objects of research, the data from two different sources was obtained. They were: (a) Farmers and (b) Bank branches operating in the area.

(a) *Farmers:* Data regarding structure of financial agencies in financing agriculture, purpose of borrowing, security offered for loans, etc., was collected personally from the beneficiaries. Information relating income position and other characteristic features were also collected.

(b) *Bank Branches:* In the selected villages, various branches of banks were contacted and information about their credit position in terms of loans advanced, securities obtained, position of recoveries and overdues etc. was collected. The data regarding repayment habits of the beneficiaries and the follow up efforts made by the branch officials was also obtained. The survey of bank branches was taken with two objectives: (i) to fill the gap owing to missing data, and (ii) to cross check the information provided by the farmers.

The above said information was collected by means of a field survey and discussions with farmers as well as with branch managers in villages.

For this purpose two set of questionnaires were prepared — one for the banks and the other for the farmers to arrive at some definite conclusion. Copies of these questionnaires are given in the Appendices.

Pre-testing of these questionnaires was done in village Dabler of R.S. Pura block and village Manwal of Dansal block. On this basis the schedules were modified. The modified schedules were cyclostyled and convassed personally by the researcher.

The field work was done during the months of May, June of 1988 and 1990.

After collection of the data, it was tabulated. The data so tabulated was shifted and used in the construction of tables which provided the basis for analysis.

Secondary Data

The secondary data have been collected from various publications of State Govt. Some of the important publications are:

(i) Annual Action Plan, Lead Bank Scheme 1988-89 of Jammu and Poonch Districts.

(ii) State Digest of Statistics issued by Directorate of Economics and Statistics Planning and Development Department.

(iii) Report of Agricultural Census (1985-86) Jammu and Kashmir State, issued by State Agricultural Census Commissioner.

(iv) District Census Hand-Book and various other Census reports issued by Director of Census Operation, J&K.

(v) Hand Book of Statistics (1982-83) issued by District Development Commissioner.

(vi) Economic Review of Jammu and Kashmir issued by Directorate of Economics and Statistics, Planning and Development Department.

(vii) Other small publications issued by Directorate of Information, Jammu & Kashmir.

Besides these, data was also procured from various other State Publications, Reports, Journals and Monographs.

Scope

Within a limited scope of a particular region, the study is worked out with a broader perspective on the basis of three specific indicators representing concentration of small holding, level of infrastructural facilities and level of banking industry development. This is, because of the operational difficulties in credit advancement and its utilisation pattern in the under-developed areas. For the purpose of the present study the measurement of the impact of bank loans is, therefore, attempted through the sample of farmers form activities pertaining to the bank loan.

REFERENCES

1. Cohen, R.L., *The Economics of Agriculture*, London (1959), p. 162.
2. Rules for the Conduct of Business of the J & K Central Land Mortgage Bank Ltd.
3. A.M. Probhu, "The Politics of Credit", *The Economic Times*, 29 January, 1990, p. 4.
4. *The Economic Times*, 1 November 1990, p. 1.
5. Charanjit Chanana, *Agricultural Finance in India*, p. 160.

2
AGRICULTURE SITUATION IN JAMMU AND KASHMIR

Agriculture is the mainstay of the State's economy. About 2/3 of the population lives in rural areas whose primary occupation is agriculture. Agricultural situation in the state can be seen from the following parameters:

Land-use Pattern

Total area according to village paper is 2416 thousand hectares in 1985-86. Out of which 723 thousand hectares is covered under net area sown. Net area sown represents area sown under crops and orchards.

Out of the net area sown in the state, over 326 thousand hectares (45%) is in the Kashmir Division including over 18 thousand hectares of Ladakh and Kargil districts and the remaining over 396 thousand hectares (55%) is in Jammu Division. Among districts, Jammu district contributed 17% of the total area sown in the state, followed by Baramulla (10%), Udhampur, Kathua, Anantnag and Doda (9% each), Pulwama (8%), Rajouri and Budgam (7% each), Kupwara (6%), Poonch (4%) and Srinagar (3%). Leh and Kargil districts contributed (1% each) and ranked to the bottom.

The class-wise size of holdings differed from each other. The percentage of net area sown varied from 75.64% in marginal size class holding to 36.46% in large size class holdings. The decline was quite consistent as is vividly seen from the following Table 2.1 below:

Table 2.1

Land-use Pattern by size class net area sown in 000' Ha.

Size class	*Net area sown in 000' Ha.*	*Percentage to total land use*
Marginal	253.1	75.64
Small	191.9	75.61
Semi-medium	186.1	70.73
Medium	75.2	53.84
Large	16.3	36.46
Total	722.6	70.57

Source: Agricultural Census 1985-86.

Cropping Pattern

In Jammu and Kashmir State, paddy and maize are the two principal crops grown during the kharif season. Besides, other food crops like barley, bajra, pulses, fruits, vegetables etc. are also grown while in the rabi season, wheat, oil-seeds and vegetables are the main food crops. During 1985-86, the gross cultivated/cropped area was 1093.4 thousand hectares out of which 638.7 thousand hectares was in Jammu region 422.1 thousand hectares in Kashmir region and 32.6 thousand hectares in Ladakh region.

Paddy, maize and wheat are the principal crops grown in the state. These crops together constituted about 76.60% of the total cropped area in the state and individually these contributed 27.7%, 26.6% and 22.3% for paddy, maize and wheat respectively. The area under other crops viz. fruits, oilseeds, pulses, vegetables, barley, bajra etc. was 23.4% of the total cropped area. Fruits and oilseeds continued to be the only other crops which formed somewhat significant cultivated area after the main three principal crops mentioned above.

As per Agricultural Census 1985-86, the total area under paddy in the state was estimated to be of the order of 302.8 thousand hectares of which 173.2 thousand hectares were in Kashmir region and 129.6 thousand hectares in Jammu region. In Kashmir region maize crop constituted about one-fourth of the total cropped area in the region being second largest crop in the region as also at state level. Wheat accounting for

36.79% and maize accounting for 29% of its total cropped area were the two major crops grown in the Jammu region followed by paddy which accounted for about 20% of its total cropped area.

Land Holdings

Total number of holdings in the state in 1985-86 was 1185 thousand hectares with an average holding of 0.86 hectares.

The marginal holdings accounted for the largest share (73.9%) in the total holdings followed by small holdings (15.8%), semi-medium holdings (8.3%), medium holdings (1.9%) and large size holdings (0.1%).

The marginal holdings which accounted for about 74% of total holdings had a share of hardly 33% of the total operated area; whereas the semi-medium, medium and large holdings put together accounting for 10% of the total holdings had a large share of about 43% in the total operated area.

The marginal holdings and small holdings put together formed about 90% of all operational holdings with share of hardly two-third in the total operated area in the state.

Out of the total holdings in the State, Anantnag District accounted for the largest share of 13.3% followed by Baramulla (13%) and Jammu (12.9%), Leh District accounted for the lowest share of holdings (0.9%) followed by Kargil District (1.1%).

Irrigation

The total area receiving irrigation was estimated to be about 3.14 lakh hectares which constituted 43.44% of the total net area sown of holdings in the state. The extent of holdings receiving irrigation wholly or partly was 59.79% of the total holdings. Among the districts, the maximum area receiving irrigation was 0.67 lakh hectares approximately in Jammu district and minimum was 0.04 lakh hectares approximately in Poonch district. On the other hand, Budgam district topped with 78.26% area receiving irrigation to total net area sown and Udhampur district with only 8.58% area receiving irrigation to total net area sown ranked to the bottom. The need for extension of irrigation facilities to the un-irrigated area is very much wanted.

Of the total holdings receiving irrigation at the state level over 54% received irrigation through canals followed by other sources which presumably include lift irrigation (44%). The remaining sources estimated 2% hardly viz. Tanks (over %), wells (0.32%) and Tubewells (0.48%).

New Agricultural Strategy

One of the outstanding achievements of modern agriculturist science is the development of improved varieties of seeds for different crops.

The high yielding variety programme was extended to the entire state in the year 1967-68, resulting in 85,000 tonnes of additional foodgrains.[1] The State Govt. had introduced the schemes of giving taccavi loans for purchase of fertilizers to farmers in such areas where co-operative societies were not formed. For granting these loans powers were delegated to the level of village workers.

During 1985-86 about 34.19 thousand tonnes of chemical fertilizers were distributed among the farmers. Inspite of the above improvements in agriculture, productivity is low. The State Govt. has to secure foodgrains from the centre to meet the requirements.

Implements and Machinery

It is reported that there are 2330 tractors in the State out of which 118 are registered during the year 1985-86. In addition there are other agricultural implements which may be used for mechanisation of agriculture:

1. Ploughs
2. Chaffcutters
3. Pruning scissors
4. Orchard ladders
5. Diesel and electric driven pumps
6. Paddy thresher
7. Wheat thresher
8. Maize shellers etc.

Position of Agriculture in State's Economy

Agriculture is the State's largest industry, that ought to be diversified, made so fruitful, that is also to contribute to the income of state, lessen its burden of unemployment and, if possible, contribute to its savings and help in the capital formation. Although, the share of manufacturing industries and service sector in the state, the income has been gradually increasing; yet it has not decreased the poverty-line of the farmers and, the income has gone into the hands of the favourite few. The records show that the contribution of agriculture has been efficient. The significance of agriculture in the process of economic development of the State can be gauged from the following factors:-

1. Contribution in State's income

The share of agriculture in State's incomes was as high as 56.67 per cent in 1970-71; in 1985 it was about 45 per cent; indicating, thereby, that agriculture remains the major source of income in J&K, even after more than thirty five years of economic planning. There are limitations in the working of State machinery itself. These are in terms of finance and also in terms of the shortage of the efficient and honest workers, bank-operators and administrators with all the limited resources available for investment, the agriculture continues to be the major source of income to the state. It has contributed Rs. 192 crores or 42% to the SDP during 1985-86.

The analysis of various economic activities, reveal that the economy of the State is heavily reliant on agriculture, and its allied fields. These bring about 61% of the state's income as compared to 52.1% in case of the entire country.

The revenue is raised from land, irrigation charges, tax on agriculture income etc., which facilitate the state as well as the public to keep up the balance rate of economic growth of the individual and of the society.

2. Contribution in Employment

According to latest estimate, 63.88 per cent of State's working population is employed in agriculture and allied activities. We need to facilitate the farmers and widen the scope of the agricultural sector, so as to involve more and more people in its development, and bring about a new green revolution. A provision of Rs. 15625 lakhs was allotted to this sector during the 7th Five Year Plan, resulting in the avenues of various jobs in this sector.

3. Contribution in Savings

The widening scope of agriculture sector contributes — indirectly and directly to the savings. Savings in the rural areas is estimated round about 28,281 lakh, which amounts to 29.11% of the total deposits.

4. Contribution to Capital Formation

Savings contribute to capital formation. It necessitates more and more spread of agriculture finance industries to cater the needs of the public involved in this sector. Agriculture contributes Rs. 8199 lakhs as 19.80% of the total money of the state out of it 10% loan money is invested further in this sector.

5. Contribution to Foreign Exchange

A number of agricultural commodities like seeds, honey, cottòn, grams, pulses etc. are exported from the State and earn valuable foreign exchange. According to the latest estimate, in 1986-87, 2.56 ton of agricultural seeds, 0.07 ton honey, 7.37 ton fibres, 7.82 ton cotton and 78.47 ton gram and pulses have been exported.

Position of Agricultural Finance in the State

Agriculture and finance are two coordinated factors in the evolution of prosperous economy life of the country. Outstanding advance to agriculture in the State during 1986 was recorded at Rs. 50,09,17,000 which has been gradually increasing to Rs. 75,50,55,000 during 1987, Rs. 80,06,03,000 during 1988 and Rs. 87,78,62,000 during 1989. This shows that the trend of increasing demand for agricultural finance which the intelligentsia of the State must have to fulfil the increasing future needs for the purpose of agricultural development.

The District-wise outstanding advances to agriculture in the State during 1989 was recorded at Rs. 25,59,55,000 in Srinagar, followed by in Anantnag Rs. 12,09,14,000, in Baramulla Rs. 9,60,29,000, in Jammu Rs. 9,02,30,000, in Kathua Rs. 5,23,38,000, in Udhampur Rs. 4,87,21,000, in Badgam Rs. 2,38,57,000, in Poonch Rs. 1,73,50,000, in Doda Rs. 15,44,40,000, in Ladakh Rs. 13,24,000 and in Kargil Rs. 3,18,000.

We need more and more exploration in the field and a definite scientific approach to wide its scope, finance it properly to proper and efficient persons; so that its activities are diversified in diversed channels of national prosperity and economic opulence.

We find, with the advancement of service and, the acute growth of population, the more and more dependency of agriculture, is not become only a necessity; but it has also thrown us a challenge of meeting out the exigencies of the time and save people from advancing pollution, and ecological imbalance caused by the rapid deforestation. That is the reason, why we have widened the scope of study, as far as the broader implications of agricultural finance is concerned. Therefore, within the limitations of the topic of study, we have tried here and there transcended the boundaries of a particular State; and have tried to assess the problems of Agriculture and Finance in scientific and rational terms to suit the spirit of the age.

REFERENCE

1. J & K Fact Sheet IV (Progress at a glance), published by the Department of Information, 1969, Jammu, Feb. 28, 1969, p. 9.

3

SOCIO-ECONOMIC CHARACTERISTICS OF PEOPLE IN JAMMU DIVISION

Agricultural finance is the function of socio-economic characteristics of the people living in the area of operation. These characteristics will indicate the level and nature of finance, their capacity to borrow and their ability to pay interest charges and the repayment of loans with interest.

If there is a mis-match between the financial needs of agriculturists and their socio-economic characteristics, the scheme of agricultural finance cannot be carried smoothly.

An attempt has been made in this chapter to examine the basic socio-economic characteristics of the beneficiaries (covered under survey) like distribution of population by sex and age, average family size, educational status of the population, size of holdings, extent of tenancy, types of land, economic status of the population, farm family assets and family incomes.

Sex and Age Composition

The study of population according to age and sex will prove useful to estimate the working population on the one hand and to discuss the composition of population on the other.

The distribution of sample farmers on the basis of sex and age criteria is presented in Tables 3.1 to 3.5.

Table 3.1

Distribution of population by sex and age groups in Jammu Division covered under study

Age Groups	*Males*		*Females*		*Total*	
	No.	*%*	*No.*	*%*	*No.*	*%*
0—5	63	9.06	49	8.33	112	8.73
6—15	182	26.19	165	28.06	347	27.04
16—25	163	23.45	137	23.30	300	23.38
26—35	124	17.84	106	18.03	230	17.93
36—45	85	12.23	77	13.10	162	12.63
46—59	49	7.05	33	5.61	82	6.39
60—above	29	4.17	21	3.57	50	3.90
Total	695	100.00	588	100.00	1283	100.00

Table 3.2

Distribution of population by sex and age groups Developed Area of Developed District (R.S. Pura Block)

Age Groups	*Males*		*Females*		*Total*	
	No.	*%*	*No.*	*%*	*No.*	*%*
0—5	19	10.56	13	8.84	32	9.79
6—15	39	21.67	42	28.57	81	24.77
16—25	53	29.67	48	32.65	101	30.89
26—35	19	10.55	9	6.12	28	8.56
36—45	24	10.33	21	14.29	45	13.76
46—59	14	7.78	5	3.40	19	5.81
60—above	12	6.67	9	6.12	21	6.42
Total:	180	100.00	147	100.00	327	100.00

Table 3.3

Distribution of population by sex and age groups Under-developed area of Developed District (Dansal Block)

Age Groups	*Males*		*Females*		*Total*	
	No.	*%*	*No.*	*%*	*No.*	*%*
0—5	13	7.07	8	5.67	21	6.46
6—15	56	30.44	43	30.50	99	30.46
16—25	53	28.80	40	28.37	93	28.61
26—35	21	11.41	24	17.02	45	13.85
36—45	19	10.33	16	11.35	35	10.77
46—59	15	8.15	7	4.96	22	6.77
60—above	7	3.80	3	2.13	10	3.08
Total	184	100.00	141	100.00	325	100.00

Table 3.1 indicates that majority of the family members (60%) in Jammu Division belong to the working age group of 16-59. The study further reveals that about 36% of family members fall in the age groups of 0—5 and 6—15 whereas the corresponding percentage in the age group of 60 and above is 3.90 only.

The total population covered under survey is comprised of 695 males and 588 females. It is observed that more than 60 per cent of males and females fall in the age group of 16—59. The percentage of males and females in the age groups i.e. 0—15, 6—15 and 60—above ranges between 3.57 (60—above) and 28.06 (6—15).

The participation rate according to survey is much higher than obtaining at the state level on the one hand and Jammu Division on the other. The implication of this phenomenon is that it increases the capacity to borrow and income of the beneficiaries in the region as more than one person may be earner in one household.

R.S. Pura Block

Table 3.2 indicates that out of 327 family members covered under survey in R.S. Pura block, 180 are males (55%) and 147 are females

(45%). About 59% of the total population belong to the working age group of 16—59. The proportion of dependents falling in the age group of 0-15 and 60 and above constitutes 34.6 per cent and 6.4 per cent respectively.

Dansal Block

Table 3.3 reveals that out of 325 members covered under survey in Dansal Block, 184 or 57% are males and 43% females. It is further observed from the table under reference that 60% of the total population falls in the age group of 16—59. Those who fall in the category of dependents constitute about 37% in the age groups of 0—15 and 3% in 60—above of the total population covered under survey.

Haveli Block

Table 3.4 shows that majority of family members in Haveli Block of Poonch district falls in the working age group of 16—59 which constitutes 63.5 per cent of the total family members, remaining 34.2 per cent and 2.3 per cent fall in the dependent age groups of 0—15 and 60—above respectively. The proportion of males and females among the total population of this block has been worked out at 53 and 47 respectively.

Table 3.4

Distribution of population by sex and age groups—developed area of under-developed district (Haveli block).

Age Groups	*Males*		*Females*		*Total*	
	No.	*%*	*No.*	*%*	*No.*	*%*
0—5	09	6.47	08	6.45	17	6.46
6—15	39	28.06	34	27.42	73	27.76
16—25	24	17.27	21	16.94	45	17.11
26—35	36	25.90	33	26.61	69	26.24
36—45	18	12.95	16	12.90	34	12.93
46—59	10	7.19	9	7.26	19	7.22
60—above	3	2.16	3	2.42	6	2.28
Total	139	100.00	124	100.00	263	100.00

Mendhar Block

It is observed from the table 3.6 that out of the total population covered in Mendhar block, 192 are males and 176 are females. The corresponding percentage in the working age group of 16—59 is 60 and 59 respectively. It further reveals that out of the total family members comparing males and females 60 percent of which belongs to the working age group and the balance of 36.5 per cent and 3.5 per cent belong to the dependent age groups of 0—15 and 60—above respectively.

The position regarding sex and age composition is almost the same in all the four blocks of Jammu Division. The percentage of males and females in the age group of 16—59 ranges between 60 to 64 whereas the dependents (0—15 and 60—above) ranges 40 to 36.

In a welfare society persons either too young or too old are not expected to earn their livelihood. Either they are dependents on the earning members of the family or they get pension or depend on their past savings. It is revealed from tables 3.1 to 3.5 that there is more burden of dependents on the earners.

Table 3.5

Distribution of population by Sex and Age Groups Under-developed area of under-developed district (Mendhar block).

Age Groups	*Males*		*Females*		*Total*	
	No.	*%*	*No.*	*%*	*No.*	*%*
0—5	22	11.46	20	11.36	42	11.41
6—15	48	25.00	46	26.14	94	25.54
16—25	33	17.19	28	15.91	61	16.58
26—35	48	25.00	40	22.73	88	23.91
36—45	24	12.50	24	13.64	48	13.04
46—59	10	5.20	12	6.82	22	5.99
60—above	7	3.65	6	3.41	13	3.53
Total:	192	100.00	176	100.00	368	100.00

Family Size and Availability of Land Per Capita

Since family is a basic social unit, the extent of its size gives an idea about the working force available, consumption expenditures and capacity of the family to earn, save and invest in the farming enterprise, etc. For analytical purposes, the sampled beneficiaries have been divided into five groups:

(i) *Marginal Farmers*: holding upto 2.50 acres irrigated land or upto 5.00 acres of unirrigated land.

(ii) *Small Farmers*: holding upto 2.51 acres to 5.00 acres irrigated land or from 5.01 to 10.00 acres of unirrigated land.

(iii) *Medium Farmers*: holding more than 5 acres upto 7.50 acres irrigated land or from 10.01 acres to 15.00 acres of unirrigated land.

(iv) *Large Farmers*: holding from 7.51 acres to 10.00 acres and above irrigated land or more than 15 acres of unirrigated land.

(v) *Landless Labourers*: having no land at all either leased in or owned.

Table 3.6 reveals that family size and available land per capita on an average have been worked out at 6.42 persons and 0.50 acres of land respectively. Average family size for the medium and large farmers has been computed around 8 persons which is the highest in Jammu Division, followed by marginal farmers (6.61), small farmers (6.29) and landless labourers (6.08). According to survey, land per capita in case of large farmers is the highest (1.96 acres) which is followed by medium farmers (1.13 acres), small farmers (0.78 acres) and marginal farmers (0.27 acres).

Table 3.7 reveals that in R.S. Pura block and Dansal block of Jammu district, average family size for the medium farmers is the highest which is worked out at closer to 8 persons and 9 persons respectively. This category of farmers are not found in Haveli block of Poonch district, but in the Mendhar block of Poonch district the average family size in case of medium farmers is worked out at 7 persons.

In case of large farmers the average family size has been computed at 8 persons in R.S. Pura block and 4 persons in Dansal block of Jammu district. In case of Poonch district there is hardly any farmer who comes under this category.

Table 3.6

Average Family size and Land Per Capita

Size Groups	*Family Size*	*Land per capita*
Marginal Farmers	6.61	.27
Small Farmers	6.29	.78
Medium Farmers	7.71	1.13
Large Farmers	7.65	1.96
Landless Labourers	6.08	—
All Farmers	6.42	.50

In the other sized groups of R.S. Pura block, average family size is the highest among landless labourers which is worked out at 6.2 persons followed by small farmers (5.9 persons), and marginal farmers (5.6 persons) conversely, in Dansal block, the family size ranges between 5.8 (small farmers) and 6.6 (marginal farmers) whereas in Haveli block of Poonch district, the average family size in case of marginal farmers and landless labourers is worked out at 5.3 persons and 4.67 persons respectively. In Mendhar block of Poonch district, it has been worked out at 8 in case of small farmers and landless labourers followed by marginal farmers (7.3 persons) and medium farmers (6.67 persons).

Average family size in Mendhar block is the highest to the tune of 7.31 persons followed by R.S. Pura block (6.54 persons), Dansal block (6.50 persons) and Haveli block (5.26 persons).

The table under reference further reveals that in R.S. Pura block, land per capita is the highest (1.88 acres) in case of big farmers which is followed by the medium farmers, small farmers and marginal farmers with land per capita of 0.91, 0.64 and 0.29 acres respectively. In the Dansal block again the large farmers are having the largest land per capita i.e. 4.25 acres followed by medium farmers (1.67 acres), small farmers (0.99 acres) and marginal farmers (0.34 acres).

Table 3.7

Average Family Size and Land Per Capita of different size groups in different four blocks of Jammu Division.

Size	*Average Family Size*				*Land per Capita (in acres)*			
	Developed area (R.S. Pura Block)	*Under-developed area (Dansal Block)*	*Developed area (Haveli Block)*	*Under-developed area (Mendhar Block)*	*R.S. Pura Block*	*Dansal Block*	*Haveli Block*	*Mendhar Block*
Marginal Farmers	5.63	6.56	5.30	7.31	0.29	0.34	0.20	0.25
Small Farmers	5.87	5.83	—	8.33	0.64	0.99	—	0.74
Medium Farmers	8.00	9.00	—	6.67	0.91	1.67	—	1.28
Large Farmers	7.88	4.00	—	—	1.88	4.25	—	—
Landless Labourers	6.20	6.00	4.67	8.00	—	—	—	—
All Farmers	6.54	6.50	5.26	7.31	0.96	0.50	0.19	0.33

In Mendhar block of Poonch district, land per capita is calculated at 1.28 acres in case of medium farmers which is followed by small farmers (0.74 acres), marginal farmers (0.25 acres). Whereas in the developed area (Haveli block) of Poonch district only marginal farmers are found with smallest land per capita of 0.20 acres.

Taking all farmers together land per capita in R.S. Pura and Dansal blocks of Jammu district is worked out to 0.96 acres and 0.50 acres respectively. Whereas in Haveli block and Mendhar block of Poonch district, land per capita is computed at 0.19 acres and 0.33 acres respectively. It may be stated that land per capita in Haveli block is the lowest in spite of the lowest family size in this block. It means the lowest land per capita because all beneficiaries are marginal farmers. Therefore, much more attention of the State Govt. to increase agricultural productivity is required in this block of Jammu Division.

Educational Status

Extent of literacy determines the qualitative aspect of the population. It is believed that there is close relationship between the level of education of agriculturists and the use of agricultural credit. A literate person uses finance in a more systematic way as compared to the illiterate person.

The literacy level of the sample families is presented in Table 3.8. Matriculation is the highest literacy level of the heads of the families covered under survey.The sample reveals that 69.5% of the beneficiaries are illiterate and out of the remaining, 13.5% are educated upto primary level, 26% have acquired knowledge upto middle level and only 4% are matriculates.

Across the blocks, in R.S. Pura block 48 per cent are literate. In other blocks of Jammu Division, 44% are literate in Dansal Block, 18 per cent in Mendhar block and 12 per cent in Haveli block.

Table 3.9 depicts the educational status of population covered under survey in Jammu Division. It is observed that out of 1283 persons covered under survey. 25 per cent are literate and the remaining of 75% are illiterate. Among the literate population there are 218 males and the remaining 101 females. It further reveals that out of literate population

Table 3.8

Distribution of Head of Family by level of Education in Jammu Division covered under survey.

Educational Status	*Developed Area (Jammu District)*				*Under-developed Area (Poonch District)*				*Total No. of heads*	*%age to total*
	R.S. Pura Block Developed Area		*Dansal Block Under-developed Area*		*Haveli Block Developed Area*		*Mendhar Block Under-developed Area*			
	No. of heads	*%age to total*	*No. of heads*	*%age to total*	*No. of heads*	*%age to total*	*No. of heads*	*%age to total*		
Illiterate	26	52.00	28	56.00	44	88.00	41	82.00	139	69.5
Primary	09	18.00	09	18.00	4	8.00	5	10.00	27	13.5
Middle	12	24.00	10	20.00	2	4.00	2	4.00	26	13.0
Matric	3	6.00	3	6.00	—	—	2	4.00	08	4.0
Total:	50	100.00	50	100.00	50	100.00	50	100.00	200	100.00

Table 3.9

Educational Status of sample population in Jammu Division.

Educational Status	*Males*			*Females*			*Total*		
	No.	*%age*	*%age excluding illiterates*	*No.*	*%age*	*%age excluding illiterates*	*No.*	*%age*	*%age excluding illiterates*
Illiterate	477	68.63	—	487	82.83	—	964	75.14	—
Primary	84	12.09	38.53	54	9.18	53.47	138	10.75	43.26
Middle	81	11.65	37.16	26	4.42	25.74	107	8.34	33.54
Matric	49	7.05	22.48	19	3.23	18.81	68	5.30	21.32
Graduate	04	0.58	1.83	02	0.34	1.98	06	0.47	1.88
Total:	695	100.00	100.00	588	100.00	100.00	1283	100.00	100.00

0.47 per cent are graduates, 5.30 per cent matriculates, 8.54 per cent middle passed and 10.75 per cent had got primary education.

Table under reference further shows that out of educated male population, 12.09 per cent are educated upto primary level, 11.65 per cent upto middle level, 7.05 per cent upto matriculation and 0.58 per cent upto graduation level. Among literate female population, 9.18 per cent are educated upto primary level, 4.42 per cent middle level, 3.23 per cent upto matriculation level and 0.34 per cent upto graduation level.

In short, it may be stated that majority of the educated, 78 per cent are educated upto primary and middle level and another 20 per cent are educated upto matriculation level. The percentage of graduate among the literate population is only 2 per cent.

R.S. Pura Block

Table 3.10 reveals that in R.S. Pura Block, the literacy rate is 38.23 per cent which is the highest among the four blocks of Jammu Division. Out of the total population, 14.68 per cent are educated upto primary level, 14.68 per cent upto middle level, 7.95 per cent upto matriculation level and only 0.92 per cent upto graduate level. Literacy rate among males and females in this block has been worked out at 48.8 per cent and 24.17 per cent respectively.

Dansal Block

Table 3.11 represents that in Dansal Block of Jammu district 31.38 per cent of the population is literate out of which 11.38 per cent acquired the knowledge upto primary level, 9.85 per cent upto middle and the remaining 10.15 per cent upto matriculation level. Table under reference further reveals that 39.67 per cent among males and 20.58 per cent among females are literate.

Haveli Block

Table 3.12 shows that in Haveli block of Poonch district, 9.88 per cent of the population is literate. 6.46 per cent are educated upto primary level and only 3.42 per cent upto middle. This shows that literacy rate is the worst in this block as compared to other blocks of Jammu division. Further, literacy rate among males and females has been estimated at 12.95 per cent and 6.45 per cent respectively.

Table 3.10

Educational Status of Population in Developed Area of developed district (R.S. Pura Block—Jammu District)

Educational Status	*Males*			*Females*			*Total*		
	No.	*%age*	*%age excluding illiterates*	*No.*	*%age*	*%age excluding illiterates*	*No.*	*%age*	*%age excluding illiterates*
Illiterate	92	51.11	—	110	74.83	—	202	61.77	—
Primary	30	16.67	34.09	18	12.25	48.65	48	14.68	38.40
Middle	38	21.11	43.18	10	6.80	27.03	48	14.68	38.40
Matric	18	10.00	20.46	08	5.44	21.62	26	7.95	20.80
Graduate	02	1.11	2.27	01	0.68	2.70	03	0.92	2.40
Total:	180	100.00	100.00	147	100.00	100.00	327	100.00	100.00

Table 3.11

Educational Status of Population in Under-developed area of developed district (Dansal Block—Jammu District)

Educational Status	*Males*			*Females*			*Total*		
	No.	*%age*	*%age excluding illiterates*	*No.*	*%age*	*%age excluding illiterates*	*No.*	*%age*	*%age excluding illiterates*
Illiterate	111	60.63	—	112	79.42	—	223	68.62	—
Primary	22	11.95	30.14	15	10.64	51.72	37	11.38	36.28
Middle	26	14.13	35.62	6	4.25	20.70	32	9.85	31.37
Matric	25	13.59	34.25	8	5.67	27.58	33	10.15	32.35
Graduate	—	—	—	—	—	—	—	—	—
Total:	184	100.00	100.00	141	100.00	100.00	325	100.00	100.00

Mendhar Block

Table 3.13 shows that in Mendhar block of Poonch district, literacy rate is 17.94 per cent. 9.78 per cent are educated upto primary level, 4.89 per cent middle, 2.45 per cent matriculates and 0.82 per cent are graduates. So far education of males and females is concerned, the table under reference reveals that 20.37 per cent among males and 15.34 per cent among females are literate.

Distribution of Land Holdings

The sample beneficiaries are divided into five groups according to size of land holdings namely marginal farmers, small farmers, medium farmers, large farmers and landless labourers.

Table 3.14 shows that out of 200 beneficiaries covered under survey, 147 fall in the category of marginal farmers, 17 each in the category of small farmers and large farmers, 7 in the category of medium farmers and the remaining 12 in the category of landless labourers. Table under reference further shows that farmers covered under survey have in possession about 645.01 acres of land in total, with an average holding size of 3.43 acres of land. Whereas the average holding of large farmers has been worked out at 14.16 acres, it is followed by the medium farmers (8.73 acres), small farmers (4.91 acres) and marginal farmers (1.67 acres). In other words 39.42 per cent of the total holdings is held by large farmers, 38.14 per cent by marginal farmers, 12.95 per cent by small farmers and 9.48 per cent by medium farmers.

R.S. Pura Block

Table 3.15 discloses that majority of the farmers in developed area (R.S. Pura block) of developed district (Jammu) belong to the category of marginal farmers. Out of 50 farmers covered under survey 19(38%) fall in the group size of 0—2.20 acres (marginal farmers), 2(4%) in 5.01 acres to 7.50 acres group (medium farmers) 16 (32%) in 7.51 and 10 acres groups (large farmers). Only 5(10%) fall in the group of landless labourers.

The table under reference further reveals that large farmers have the largest holding i.e. 73.92 per cent with average size of holding of 14.83 acres which is followed by the marginal farmers, small farmers and medium farmers with average size of holdings 1.60 acres, 3.78 acres and 7.25 acres respectively.

Table 3.12

Educational Status of Population in Developed area of Under-developed District (Haveli Block - Poonch District)

Educational Status	*Males*			*Females*			*Total*		
	No.	*%age*	*%age excluding illiterates*	*No.*	*%age*	*%age excluding illiterates*	*No.*	*%age*	*%age excluding illiterates*
Illiterate	121	87.05	—	116	93.55	—	237	90.12	—
Primary	12	8.63	66.67	5	4.03	62.5	17	6.46	65.38
Middle	6	4.32	33.33	3	2.42	37.5	09	3.42	34.62
Matric	—	—	—	—	—	—	—	—	—
Graduate	—	—	—	—	—	—	—	—	—
Total:	139	100.00	100.00	124	100.00	100.00	263	100.00	100.00

Table 3.13

Educational Status of Population in underdeveloped area of underdeveloped district (Mendhar Block - Poonch District)

Educational Status	*Males*			*Females*			*Total*		
	No.	*%age*	*%age excluding illiterates*	*No.*	*%age*	*%age excluding illiterates*	*No.*	*%age*	*%age excluding illiterates*
Illiterate	153	79.69	—	149	84.66	—	302	82.06	—
Primary	20	10.42	51.28	16	9.09	59.26	36	9.78	54.54
Middle	11	5.73	28.21	7	3.98	25.93	18	4.89	27.27
Matric	6	3.12	15.38	3	1.70	11.11	9	2.45	13.64
Graduate	2	1.04	5.13	1	0.57	3.70	3	0.82	4.55
Total:	192	100.00	100.00	176	100.00	100.00	368	100.00	100.00

Table 3.14

Distribution of Selected farms and area in Jammu Division covered under survey.

(in Acres)

Size Group	*No. of farms*	*Total area of operational holding in acres*	*Percentage of total operational area*	*Average size of holding excluding landless labourer*
Marginal Farmers	147	246.12	38.14	1.67
Small Farmers	17	83.51	12.95	4.91
Medium Farmers	7	61.13	9.48	8.73
Large Farmers	17	254.25	39.42	14.96
Landless Labourers	12	—	—	—
Total:	200	645.01	100.00	3.43

Dansal Block

Table 3.16 reveals that majority of the farmers in under developed area (Dansal Block) of developed district (Jammu) belong to the category of marginal farmers. Out of 50 farmers covered under survey in this block, 39 (78%) fall in the category of marginal farmers, 6 (12%) in small farmers, 2 (4%) in medium farmers, 1 (2%) in large farmers and 2 (4%) fall in the group of landless labourers.

Table under reference further shows that marginal farmers have the largest holding of (54.74 per cent) 88 acres with the smallest average size of holding of 2.26 acres. It is followed by small farmers, medium farmers and large farmers, who own 21.62 per cent, 13.06 per cent and 10.58 per cent of the total land with average holding of 5.79 acres, 10.50 acres and 17.00 acres respectively.

Table 3.15

Distribution of Selected Farms and Area in Developed Area of Developed District (R.S. Pura Block—Jammu District)

(in Acres)

Size Group	*No. of farms*	*Total area of operational holdings*	*Percentage of total operational holdings*	*Average size of holding excluding area*
Marginal Farmers	19	30.50	9.76	1.60
Small Farmers	8	30.25	9.68	3.78
Medium Farmers	2	14.50	4.64	7.25
Large Farmers	16	237.25	73.92	14.83
Landless Labourers	5	—	—	—
Total:	50	312.50	100.00	6.94

Table 3.16

Distribution of Selected Farms and Area in Underdeveloped area of developed district (Dansal block—Jammu District)

(in Acres)

Size Group	*No. of farms*	*Total area of operational holdings*	*Percentage to total operational area*	*Average size of holding area*
Marginal Farmer	39	88.00	54.74	2.26
Small Farmer	6	34.75	21.62	5.79
Medium Farmer	2	21.00	13.06	10.50
Large Farmer	1	17.00	10.58	17.00
Landless Labourer	2	—	—	—
Total:	50	160.75	100.00	3.35

Haveli Block

Table 3.17 shows that in Haveli block of Poonch district only two categories of beneficiaries exist, one in marginal farmers and the other landless labourers. The former constitute (94%) and the latter (6%) of the total farmers covered under study.

Table under reference further shows that 100 per cent area of operational holdings is occupied by marginal farmers with total operational area of 49.91 acres. This gives an average holding size of 1.06 acres which is the lowest in the category of marginal farmers as compared with the marginal farmers of other blocks.

Table 3.17

Distribution of Selected Farms and Area in Developed Area of Under-developed District (Haveli Block—Poonch District) according to Type and Size

(In Acres)

Size Group	*No. of farms*	*Total area of operational holdings*	*Percentage to total operational area*	*Average size of holding area*
Marginal Farmers	47	49.91	100.00	1.06
Small Farmers	—	—	—	—
Medium Farmers	—	—	—	—
Large Farmers	—	—	—	—
Landless Labourers	03	—	—	—
Total:	50	49.91	100.00	1.06

Mendhar Block

Table 3.18 indicates that there are 42 (84%) marginal farmers, 3 (6%) small farmers, 3 (6%) medium farmers, 2 (4%) landless labourers and no large farmers in this block.

Table 3.18 further reveals that 63.78 per cent of the total land covered under survey in this block is occupied by marginal farmers with average size of holding of 1.85 acres. Similarly 15.19 per cent with average size of holding of 6.17 acres by small farmers and 21.03 per cent with an average size of holding of 8.54 acres by the medium farmers.

In short, tables from 3.15 to 3.18 show that whereas large farmers own about 76 per cent of the total operational holdings covered under survey in Rs. Pura block, their counterparts in Dansal Block own 10.58 per cent. On the contrary, marginal farmers account for 54.74 per cent of the total operational holdings in Dansal block as against only 9.76 per cent in R.S. Pura block. 100 per cent of operational holdings in Haveli block and 64% in Mendhar Block are owned by the marginal farmers.

Table 3.18

Distribution of Selected Farms and Area in under-developed area of under-developed district (Mendhar Block - Poonch District) according to Type and Size

(in Acres)

Size Group	*No. of farms*	*Total area of operational holdings*	*Percentage to total operational area*	*Average size of holding area*
Marginal Farmers	42	77.71	63.78	1.85
Small Farmers	3	18.51	15.19	6.17
Medium Farmers	3	25.63	21.03	8.54
Large Farmers	-	—	—	—
Landless Labourers	2	—	—	—
Total:	50	121.85	100.00	2.54

Extent of Tenancy

Abolition of tenancy has been advocated by many experts in order to end the scope for exploitation. In Jammu division the number of occupancy tenants is comparatively smaller and they cultivate a very small portion of the total area. The great majority of the tenants are, tenants at will, who pay half the produce to the landlord and have no other rights whatsoever. However, tenancy is rising because of the following two reasons:

(i) In theory a farmer is supposed to own land not more than the statutory limit but in actual practice a few farmers possess much more land that they could manage. They are able to fulfil statutory conditions by distributing land among different household members fradulently. In actual practice it is under the charge of a single owner. Under such circumstances most of them fail to manage the whole land with the result that they sublet it to someone else. This gave rise to tenancy on a large scale.

(ii) Tenancy is rising, because of machinery purchased by big and medium farmers through bank loans. Some of them are willing to take land on tenancy to get full use of their machinery on land and enable themself for repayment of loans borrowed for the purpose.

The difference in the structure of cultivated holdings in terms of land owned and taken on lease may be important. This is because the nature of interest in the land not only affects the inclination to carry out long-term projects on land but it also has an important bearing on the borrowing of agricultural finance.

Table 3.19 shows that out of 200 farmers, 164 are owner cultivators, followed by owner/tenants (14), landless labourers (12), owner/landlords (7) and purely tenants (3). Out of 164 owner cultivators, 141 are marginal farmers, 15 small farmers, 3 medium farmers and 5 large farmers. Similarly out of 14 owner/tenants, 10 are big farmers, 2 medium farmers and 2 marginal farmers. All the tenants are among the marginal farmers.

Table 3.19 further shows that highest rate is 72 per cent which exists among the large farmers, followed by medium farmers (50 per cent), small farmers (12 per cent) and marginal farmers (4 per cent).

An examination of the data in table 3.19 shows that the proportion of land taken on lease generally increased with the increase in the size of cultivated holdings and consequently, it is at a substantially higher level among large and medium farmers, which constitute to an average of 5.03 acres and 1.21 acres respectively. On the other hand, the proportion of the land owned in the cultivation holdings is the highest in case of marginal farmers. The percentage being 95.81 of their total holdings, which is closely followed by small farmers (95.11) medium farmers (88.13) and large farmers (51.62).

Table under reference further shows that out of average holdings of 3.43 acres, average owner cultivating is 2.67 acres, leased in holdings 0.55 acres and leased out holdings 0.21 acres.

R.S. Pura Block

Table 3.20 displays that in R.S. Pura block, out of 50 beneficiaries, 50 per cent are owner cultivators, 28 per cent owner/tenants, 6 per cent each of purely tenants and owner/landlord and the remaining 10 per cent are landless labourers. It further describes that out of 19 marginal farmers 73.68 per cent are owner cultivators, 15.79 per cent purely tenants and 10.53 per cent owner/tenants. Similarly among 16 big farmers 62.5 per cent are tenants, 18.75 per cent each of owner cultivators and owner/landlord, 100 per cent of small farmers are owner cultivators whereas 100 per cent of medium farmers are owner/tenants.

Table 3.21 reveals that in R.S. Pura block the average size of cultivated holding has been worked out at 4.19 acres, 2.32 acres and 0.43 acre in terms of land owned, leased in an leased out respectively. This gives an average holding size of 6.94 acres. It further shows that small farmers have own cultivating holdings of 100 per cent, followed by marginal farmers (78.75 per cent) large farmers (53.60%) and medium farmers (51%). On the other hand, land leased in is the highest in case of medium farmers, which is worked out at 50 per cent of their total holdings, followed by big farmers (38.17 per cent) and marginal farmers (21.25%).

Dansal Block

Table 3.22 presents that in Dansal block 86 per cent are owner cultivators, 10 per cent owner/landlords and 4 per cent landless labourers. There is no one in the category of owner/tenants and purely tenants. Among owner cultivators, 100 per cent are big farmers, followed by marginal farmers (97.44) and small farmers (66.67). Remaining 2.56 per cent among marginal farmers and 37.33 per cent among small farmers are owner/landlords.

Table 3.19

Extent of tenancy: No. of farms and area per farm in Jammu Division

(in Acres)

Size Group	Purely owner cultivators	Purely owner cultivators and also leased in land	Farmers not owner cultivators and also leased in land	Farmers owner cultivators and leased out land	Landless labourers	Total	Area per farm*			
							Purely own cultivating holdings	Area leased in	Area leased out	Total
Marginal Farmers	141 (95.92)	2 (1.36)	3 (2.04)	1 (0.68)	—	1.47 (100.00)	1.60 (95.81)	0.04 (2.39)	0.03 (10.80)	1.67 (100.00)
Small Farmers	15 (88.24)	—	—	2 (11.76)	—	17 (100.00)	4.67 (95.11)	—	0.24 (4.89)	4.91 (100.00)
Medium Farmers	3 (50.00)	2 (33.33)	—	1 (16.67)	—	06 (100.00)	8.98 (88.13)	1.21 (11.87)	—	10.19 (100.00)
Large Farmers	5 (27.78)	10 (55.55)	—	3 (16.67)	—	18 (100.00)	7.34 (51.98)	5.03 (35.62)	1.75 (12.39)	14.12 (100.00)
Landless Labourers	—	—	—	—	12	12 (100.00)	—	—	—	—
Total: (Average)	164 (82.00)	14 (7.00)	3 (1.5)	7 (3.5)	12 (6.00)	200 (100.00)	2.67 (77.84)	0.55 (16.04)	0.21 (6.12)	3.43 (100.00)

Note: Figures in brackets represent respective percentages to row totals.

Table 3.20

Extent of Tenancy: No. of Farmers in Developed area of developed district (R.S. Pura block—Jammu District)

(in Acres)

Size Group	*Purely owner cultivators*	*Purely owner cultiva-tors and leasing in land*	*Farmers not owner cultivator and also leasing in land*	*Farmers owner cultivators and also leasing out land*	*Landless labourer*	*Total*
Marginal Farmers	14 (73.68)	2 (10.53)	3 (15.79)	—	—	19 (100.00)
Small Farmers	8 (100.00)	—	—	—	—	8 (100.00)
Medium Farmers	—	2 (100.00)	—	—	—	2 (100.00)
Large Farmers	3 (18.75)	10 (62.5)	—	3 (18.75)	—	16 (100.00)
Landless Labourers	—	—	—	—	5 (100.00)	5 (100.00)
Total:	25 (50.00)	14 (28.00)	3 (6.00)	3 (6.00)	5 (10.00)	50 (100.00)

Table 3.21
Extent of Tenancy: Area per farm in acres in developed area of developed district (R.S. Pura Block—Jammu District)

(in Acres)

Size Groups	*Purely own cultivating holding*	*Area leased in*	*Area leased out*	*Total*
Marginal Farmers	1.26	0.34	—	1.60
	(78.75)	(21.25)		(100.00)
Small Farmers	3.78	—	—	3.78
	(100.00)			(100.00)
Medium Farmers	3.63	3.62	—	7.25
	(50.00)	(50.00)		(100.00)
Large Farmers	7.95	5.66	1.22	14.83
	(53.60)	(38.17)	(8.23)	(100.00)
Landless Labourers	—	—	—	—
Average:	4.19	2.32	0.43	6.94
	(60.37)	(33.43)	(6.19)	(100.00)

Note: Figures in brackets are respective percentages in row totals.

Table 3.23 explains that in Dansal block out of 3.35 acres of an average holdings, 0.41 acres have been leased out. Agriculture in this block is risky because of its dependence on monsoon as such no one has leased in land. It is very significant to note here, that in this block, big farmers have leased out much of their holdings (70.59 per cent) instead of leased in as it is in the R.S. Pura block. It is because of hilly area where agriculture depends on monsoon and heavy machinery like tractors are not much in use, hence they need not to leased in land. On the contrary, they leased out their land, even marginal and small farmers have leased out to the extent of 4.42 per cent and 11.57 per cent of their respective holdings.

Table 3.22

Extent of Tenancy: No. of farms in underdeveloped area of developed district (Dansal Block—Jammu District)

(in Acres)

Size Group	*Purely owner cultivators*	*Purely owner cultivators and also leasing in land*	*Farmers not owner cultivators and leasing in land*	*Farmers owner cultivators and also leased out land*	*Landless labourers*	*Total*
Marginal Farmers	38 (97.44)	—	—	1 (2.56)	—	39 (100.00)
Small Farmers	4 (66.67)	—	—	2 (37.33)	—	6 (100.00)
Medium Farmers	—	—	—	2 (100.00)	—	2 (100.00)
Large Farmers	1 (100.00)	—	—	—	—	1 (100.00)
Landless Labourers	—	—	—	—	2 (100.00)	2 (100.00)
Total:	43 (86.00)	—	—	5 (10.00)	2 (4.00)	50 (100.00)

Table 3.23

Extent of Tenancy: Area of farm in acres in underdeveloped area of developed district (Dansal Block—Jammu District)

(in Acres)

Size Groups	*Purely own cultivating holdings*	*Area leased in*	*Area leased out*	*Total area*
Marginal Farmers	2.16	—	0.10	2.26
	(95.58)		(4.42)	(100.00)
Small Farmers	5.12	—	0.67	5.79
	(88.43)		(11.57)	(100.00)
Medium Farmers	10.50	—	—	10.50
	(100.00)			(100.00)
Large Farmers	5.00	—	12.00	17.00
	(29.41)		(70.59)	(100.00)
Landless Labourers	—	—	—	—
Total:	2.94	—	0.41	3.35
	(87.76)		(12.29)	(100.00)

Haveli Block

Table 3.24 reveals that the tenancy position in Haveli block is somewhat different to the tenancy position in R.S. Pura block and Dansal block. There is no tenancy at all in this block. This is not because of a very good system of land tenure, it is because of a very small size of holdings, hilly area, dependence of agriculture on monsoon and less awareness of the use of new technology. Out of 50 beneficiaries covered under survey, 94 per cent are owner cultivators and the remaining 6 per cent are landless labourers. No one has either leased out or leased in any land in this block. Further, table 3.25 depicts that 100 per cent of the holdings are owned by cultivators.

Table 3.24

Extent of Tenancy: No. of farmers in developed area of underdeveloped district (Haveli Block—Poonch District)

(in Acres)

Size Group	*Purely owner cultivators*	*Purely owner cultivators and leasing in land*	*Farmers not cultivators leasing in land*	*Farmers owner and also leasing out land*	*Landless labourers*	*Total*
Marginal Farmers	47 (100.00)	—	—	—	—	47 (100.00)
Small Farmers	—	—	—	—	—	—
Medium Farmers	—	—	—	—	—	—
Large Farmers	—	—	—	—	—	—
Landless Labourers	—	—	—	—	3 (100.00)	3 (100.00)
Total:	47 (94.00)	—	—	—	3 (6.00)	50 (100.00)

Table 3.25

Extent of Tenancy: Area per farm in acres in developed area of underdeveloped district (Haveli Block—Poonch District)

(in Acres)

Size Groups	*Purely owner cultivator holding*	*Area leased in*	*Area leased out*	*Total*
Marginal Farmers	1.06 (100.00)	—	—	1.06 (100.00)
Small Farmers	—	—	—	—
Medium Farmers	—	—	—	—
Large Farmers	—	—	—	—
Landless Labourers	—	—	—	—
Average:	1.06 (100.00)	—	—	1.06 (100.00)

Note: Figures in brackets are respective percentage in row totals.

Mendhar Block

Table 3.26 reveals that tenancy position of Mendhar block is almost the same as it is in Haveli block, that there is no tenancy. Out of 50 beneficiaries, 96 per cent are owner cultivators and the remaining 4 per cent are landless labourers. Similarly, table 3.27 reveals that 100 per cent of the holdings of all the farmers are own cultivation. None of them have leased in or leased out in this block.

In conclusion, it is stated that there was no such farmer who has taken land on lease for cultivation in all the blocks except R.S. Pura Block. It is because of small size of holdings on the one hand and dependence of agriculture on monsoon on the other.

Land Use Pattern

For study purposes, only Net area sown is taken into consideration i.e. classification of operational holdings which is cultivable and non-cultivable into irrigated and unirrigated land.

Table 3.26

Extent of Tenancy: No. of farms in under-developed area of under-developed district (Mendhar Block—Poonch District)

(in Acres)

Size Group	*Purely owner cultivators*	*Purely owner cultivator and also leasing in land*	*Farmers not owner cultivator and leasing in land*	*Farmers owner cultivators and also leasing out land*	*Landless labourers*	*Total*
Marginal Farmers	42 (100.00)	—	—	—	—	42 (100.00)
Small Farmers	3 (100.00)	—	—	—	—	03 (100.00)
Medium Farmers	3 (100.00)	—	—	—	—	03 (100.00)
Large Farmers	—	—	—	—	—	—
Landless labourers	—	—	—	—	2 (100.00)	02 (100.00)
Total:	48 (96.00)	—	—	—	2 (4.00)	50 (100.00)

Note: Figures in brackets represent respective percentage to row totals.

Classification of land is important for knowing and assessing financial needs of the farmers for use and purchase of HYV seeds, pump sets, etc. to improve upon their economic conditions.

Table 3.27

Extent of Tenancy: Area per farm in acres in under-developed area (in acres) (Mendhar Block - Poonch District)

(in Acres)

Size Groups	*Purely own cultivating holding*	*Area leased in*	*Area leased out*	*Total area*
Marginal Farmers	1.85	—	—	1.85
	(100.00)			(100.00)
Small Farmers	6.17	—	—	6.17
	(100.00)			(100.00)
Medium Farmers	8.54	—	—	8.54
	(100.00)			(100.00)
Large Farmers	—	—	—	—
Landless Labourers	—	—	—	—
Total:	2.54 (100.00)	—	—	2.54 (100.00)

Note: Figures in brackets are respective percentages in row totals.

It is learnt from the table 3.28 that out of the total operational holdings covered under survey, 51.60 per cent of which have been irrigated, 45.77 per cent unirrigated and remaining 2.63 per cent uncultivated unirrigated land. The unirrigated land is only rain-fed land. In the absence of rains when drought and famine occurs the owner of such land are left with a number of problems.[1]

Table under reference further shows that out of 332.89 acres of irrigated land, large farmers have acquired 228.25 acres, followed by the marginal farmers (49.01 acres), small farmers (30.50 acres) and medium farmers (25.13 acres). The ratio of irrigated and unirrigated land is worked out at 16:1 in case of large farmers and 1:4 in case of marginal farmers. This shows that much of irrigated and less of unirrigated land is acquired by large farmers whereas less of irrigated and much of unirrigated land is acquired by the marginal farmers. It means that problems of drought, famines, floods etc. are generally faced by the marginal farmers because much of their land is rainfed (unirrigated).

Table 3.28

Classification of land: by size of operational holdings of selected households from whole of Jammu Division (in acres)

Size Groups	*Operational Holdings*				*Total*
	Cultivated		*Uncultivated*		
	Irrigated	*Unirrigated*	*Irrigated*	*Unirrigated*	
Marginal Farmers	49.01	194.86	—	2.25	246.12
Small Farmers	30.50	51.01	—	2.00	83.51
Medium Farmers	25.13	36.00	—	—	61.13
Large Farmers	228.25	14.00	—	12.00	254.25
Landless Labourers	—	—	—	—	—
Average	1.77 (51.60)	1.57 (45.77)		0.09 (2.63)	3.43 (100.00)

R.S. Pura Block

Table 3.29 represents the land use pattern of R.S. Pura block which shows that out of 6.94 acres of average holdings, 6.67 acres have been irrigated and the rest of 0.27 acres unirrigated. In other words an average cultivator of this block have more than 96 per cent of irrigated land and a little less than 4 per cent of unirrigated land. It is also observed from the table 3.29 that out of the total irrigated land of 300.25 acres, big farmers have acquired the highest to the tune of 228.25 acres, followed by marginal farmers (30.25 acres), small farmers (27.25 acres) and medium farmers (14.50 acres). Farmers of this block by and large have possessed the irrigated lands. Only 3.89% of the land possessed by them is unirrigated. The proportion of unirrigated land varies between the minimum of 0.82 per cent under marginal farmers and the maximum of about 10 per cent under small farmers.

Table 3.29

Classification of land: by size of operational holdings of selected households from developed area of developed district (R.S. Pura Block—Jammu District)

(in Acres)

Size Groups	*Operational Holdings*				*Total*
	Cultivated		*Uncultivated*		
	Irrigated	*Unirrigated*	*Irrigated*	*Unirrigated*	
Marginal Farmers	30.25	0.25	—	—	30.50
Small Farmers	27.25	3.00	—	—	30.25
Medium Farmers	14.50	—	—	—	14.25
Large Farmers	228.25	9.00	—	—	237.25
Landless labourers	—	—	—	—	—
Average	6.67 (96.11)	0.27 (3.89)	—	—	6.94 (100.00)

Dansal Block

Table 3.30 shows that an average farmer has 3.35 acres of land in this block, out of which he has 2.81 acres of unirrigated land, 0.29 acres uncultivable unirrigated and 0.25 acres irrigated. In other words much of land (84%) in this block is unirrigated and less of land (8%) is irrigated. This shows that land use pattern in this block is the reverse to the land use pattern in R.S. Pura block. Table 3.30 further reveals that marginal farmers of this block have only 6 acres of irrigated land as against of 82 acres of unirrigated land. Similarly, other categories of farmers have much of unirrigated land and less of irrigated land. Whereas large farmers have possessed whole of rainfed area out of 70.59% is uncultivated and 29.41% cultivated.

Haveli Block

Table 3.31 shows that in Haveli block, there are only marginal farmers, those have 84% of unirrigated land and only 16% of irrigated land.

Table 3.30

Classification of land: by size of holdings of selected households underdeveloped area of developed district (Dansal Block—Jammu District)

(in Acres)

Size Groups	*Operational Holdings*				*Total*
	Cultivated		*Uncultivated*		
	Irrigated	*Unirrigated*	*Irrigated*	*Unirrigated*	
Marginal Farmers	6.00	82.00	—	—	88.00
Small Farmers	2.25	30.50	—	2.00	34.75
Medium Farmers	3.75	17.25	—	—	21.00
Large Farmers	—	5.00	—	12.00	17.00
Landless Labourers	—	—	—	—	—
Average (percentage in brackets)	0.24 (4.46)	2.81 (83.88)	—	0.29 (8.16)	3.35 (100.00)

Table 3.31

Classification of land: by size of operational holding of selected households developed area (in acres)

Size Groups	*Operational Holdings*				*Total*
	Cultivated		*Uncultivated*		
	Irrigated	*Unirrigated*	*Irrigated*	*Unirrigated*	
Marginal Farmers	7.82	42.09	—	—	49.91
Small Farmers	—	—	—	—	—
Medium Farmers	—	—	—	—	—
Large Farmers	—	—	—	—	—
Landless labourers	—	—	—	—	—
Average	.17 (16.04)	.89 (83.96)	—	—	1.06 (100.00)

Mendhar Block

Table 3.32 shows that in Mendhar Block, there are marginal farmers, small farmers and medium farmers, those have 70.52 acres, 17.51 acres and 18.75 acres unirrigated land as against of only 4.94 acres, 1.00 acres and 6.88 acres of irrigated land respectively. On an average a cultivator has 87 per cent of unirrigated land, 11 per cent irrigated and 2 per cent uncultivable unirrigated land.

It may be stated on the basis of the above mentioned tables that in Dansal block of Jammu District only 8 per cent of land is irrigated which is the lowest from all the blocks covered under survey.

Table 3.32

Classification of land: by size of operational holdings of selected households from underdeveloped area (in acres)

Size Groups	*Operational Holdings*				*Total*
	Cultivated		*Uncultivated*		
	Irrigated	*Unirrigated*	*Irrigated*	*Unirrigated*	
Marginal Farmers	4.94	70.52	—	2.25	77.71
Small Farmers	1.00	17.51	—	—	18.51
Medium Farmers	6.88	18.75	—	—	25.63
Large Farmers	—	—	—	—	—
Landless labourers	—	—	—	—	—
Average	.27 (10.63)	2.22 (87.40)	—	0.05 (1.97)	2.54 (100.00)

Economic Status of the Population

In order to find out the saving and capital formation positions of the population, it is necessary to know the number of earners and dependents. More dependents cause lesser savings and due to lesser savings and inadequate capital, investment fails to pick up. The low level of investment keeps the productivity lower and hence income lower.

Table 3.33 indicates that the population of 1283 persons covered under survey has been divided among earners and dependents according to economic status. There are 324 earners and 959 dependents. It means that 25.25 per cent are earners and 74.75 per cent are dependents. This shows that one earner is carrying the burden of three dependents on him.

Among medium farmers 33.33 per cent are earners followed by small farmers (31.78 per cent), large farmers (30 per cent), landless labourers (24.66 per cent) and marginal farmers (23.39 per cent).

Table 3.33

Economic Status of different Size Groups in Jammu Division

Size Groups	*Earners*		*Dependents*		*Total*	
	No.	*%age*	*No.*	*%age*	*No.*	*%age*
Marginal Farmers	215	23.39	704	76.61	919	71.63
Small Farmers	34	31.78	73	68.22	107	8.34
Medium Farmers	18	33.33	36	66.67	54	4.21
Large Farmers	39	30.00	91	70.00	130	10.13
Landless Labourers	18	24.66	55	75.34	73	5.69
Total:	324	25.25	959	74.75	1283	100.00

Economic Status of the Population in Blocks

Table 3.34 reveals that out of the total population in R.S. Pura block only 28.44 per cent are earners and the remaining 71.56 per cent are dependents on them. Whereas in Dansal block, the percentage of earners is little less than that of the R.S. Pura block which has been estimated at 23.69. The percentage of earners in Haveli and Mendhar blocks is 22.81 and 25.54 respectively.

The highest percentage of earners is among the large farmers of Dansal block i.e. 38.39. It is not because of agriculture, it is due to dependence on Govt. jobs. The percentage of earners among other categories of farmers of all the blocks ranges in between 22.49 in case of marginal farmers of Haveli block and 34.29 in case of small farmers of Dansal block.

Table 3.34

Economic Status of different size groups in four blocks of Jammu Division

Size	*R.S. Pura Block (Developed area)*				*Dansal Block (Undeveloped area)*				*Haveli Block (Developed area)*				*Mendhar Block (Undeveloped area)*			
	Earners		*Dependants*		*Earners*		*Dependants*		*Earners*		*Dependants*		*Earners*		*Dependants*	
	No.	*%*	*No.*	*%*	*No.*	*%*	*No.*	*%*	*No.*	*%*	*No.*	*%*	*No.*	*%*	*No.*	*%*
Marginal Farmers	28	26.17	79	73.83	54	21.09	202	78.91	56	22.49	193	77.51	77	25.08	230	74.92
Small Farmers	15	31.91	32	68.09	12	34.29	23	65.71	—	—	—	—	7	28.00	18	72.00
Medium Farmers	5	31.25	11	68.75	7	38.89	11	61.11	—	—	—	—	6	30.00	14	70.00
Large Farmers	38	30.16	88	69.75	1	25.00	3	75.00	—	—	—	—	—	—	—	—
Landless labourers	7	22.58	24	77.42	3	25.00	9	75.00	4	28.57	10	71.43	4	25.00	12	75.00
Total:	93	28.44	234	71.56	77	23.69	248	76.31	60	22.81	203	77.19	94	25.54	274	74.46

Farm Family Assets

Assets show the financial soundness of the farmers and their capacity to earn. Small holding of agricultural assets is a sign of earning less incomes particularly in the villages where other sources of earning income are very limited.

Agricultural finance and family assets are connected with each other. Generally farmers take loan to increase their farm assets in order to increase their farm production and with the increase in production, income rises which enhances the farm family assets. Farm family assets include value of land, farm building, farm machinery and implements, live stock etc.

Table 3.35 to 3.39 give the composition and average value of assets per family among five groups of beneficiaries.

Table 3.35 reveals that land is a major asset of the cultivators in Jammu Division. Out of the total assets on an average of per family of Rs.1,63,510.13, land consists 88.85 per cent, live stock 5.55 per cent, implements and machinery 0.60 per cent and others 0.07 per cent.

Tables 3.35 further reveals that cost of land holdings on an average comes to Rs.1,45,276.85, Farm building Rs.982.86, implements and machinery Rs.8055.64 live stock Rs.9074.73 and others Rs.120.05 per family.

Large farmers, medium farmers and small farmers have total assets on an average of per family worth Rs.13,07,895.20, Rs.4,45,007.14 and Rs.1,76,018.22 respectively, which are above the average of Rs.1,63,510 but a marginal farmer and a landless labour have assets below the average costing Rs.78,919.81 and Rs.8,676.26 respectively.

Land is the main asset for all types of farmers which ranges between 87.44 per cent to 94.94 per cent of their total assets but landless labours have live stock as a major asset which constitutes about 86 per cent of their total assets.

Farm Family Asset in Blocks

Tables 3.36 to 3.39 show that in R.S. Pura block, Dansal block, Haveli block and in Mendhar block, an average farmer excluding landless labourers have assets worth Rs.5,92,887.39, Rs.1,98,028.40, Rs.61,025.04 and Rs.1,24,928.41 respectively. Out of different types of assets, land is

Table 3.35

Per holding of farm family assets for different size holdings in Jammu Division (in Rupees)

Items	*Marginal farmers*	*Small farmers*	*Medium farmers*	*Large farmers*	*Landless labourers*	*All farmers on an combined average including landless labourers*	*All farmers on an combined average excluding landless labourers for land and farm building only*
1. Land	69,009.86	1,58,717.64	4,22,485.71	12,12,470.50	—	1,36,560.24	1,45,276.85
	(87.44)	(90.17)	(94.94)	(92.71)		(88.25)	(88.85)
2. Farm building	461.41	1,435.29	1,692.86	4,747.06	—	923.89	982.86
	(0.59)	(0.82)	(0.38)	(0.36)		(0.60)	(0.60)
3. Implements & machinery	1,176.91	2,670.59	4,007.14	80,227.71	66.67	8,055.64	8,055.64
	(1.49)	(1.52)	(0.90)	(6.13)	(0.77)	(5.21)	(4.93)
4. Live stock	8,271.63	12,605.88	16,821.43	10,450.00	7,442.92	9,074.73	9,074.73
	(10.48)	(7.16)	(3.78)	(0.80)	(85.78)	(5.86)	(5.55)
5. Others	—	588.82	—	—	1,166.67	120.05	120.05
		(0.33)			(13.45)	(0.08)	(0.07)
Total:	78,919.81 (100.00)	1,76,018.22 (100.00)	4,45,007.14 (100.00)	13,07,895.20 (100.00)	8,676.26 (100.00)	1,54,734.55 (100.00)	1,63,510.13 (100.00)

Table 3.36

Per holding of farm family assets: for different size groups in developed area of developed district (R.S. Pura Block—Jammu District) (in rupees)

Items	*Marginal farmers*	*Small farmers*	*Medium farmers*	*Large farmers*	*Landless labourers*	*All farmers on an combined average including landless labourers*	*All farmers on an combined average excluding landless labourers for land and farm building only*
1. Land	1,28,421 (94.94)	3,02,500 (94.46)	5,80,000 (99.01)	11,86,250 (92.54)	—	5,00,000 (93.10)	5,55,555.55 (93.71)
2. Farm building	854.08 (0.63)	1368.06 (0.43)	3000.00 (0.51)	4856.00 (0.38)	—	2217.44 (0.41)	2463.82 (0.42)
3. Implements & machinery	445.00 (0.33)	550.00 (0.17)	300.00 (0.05)	79,716.94 (6.23)	90.00 (1.37)	25,787.52 (4.80)	25,787.52 (4.35)
4. Live stock	5284.21 (3.91)	14,631.25 (4.57)	2525.00 (0.43)	10,915.63 (0.85)	3875.00 (59.03)	8490.50 (1.58)	8490.50 (1.43)
5. Others	263.16 (0.19)	1,187.50 (0.37)	—	—	2600.00 (39.60)	550.00 (0.10)	550.00 (0.09)
Total	1,35,267.45 (100.00)	3,20,236.85 (100.00)	5,85,825 (100.00)	12,81,738.50 (100.00)	6565 (100.00)	5,37,045.46 (100.00)	5,92,547.30 (100.00)

Table 3.37

Per holding of farm family assets of different size holds: in underdeveloped areas of developed district (Dansal Block—Jammu District) (in rupees)

Items	*Marginal farmers*	*Small farmers*	*Medium farmers*	*Large farmers*	*Landless labourers*	*All farmers on an combined average including landless labourers*	*All farmers on an average excluding landless labourers*
1. Land	1,07,230.76 (91.64)	2,66,000.00 (94.50)	7,56,000.00 (98.09)	16,32,000.00 (94.53)	—	1,78,440.00 (93.65)	1,85,875.00 (93.86)
2. Farm building	1,094.87 (0.94)	2,050.00 (0.73)	2,500.00 (0.32)	3,000.00 (0.17)	—	1,260.00 (0.66)	1,312.50 (0.66)
3. Implements & machinery	1,309.87 (1.12)	6,716.67 (2.39)	3,350.00 (0.44)	85,400.00 (5.12)	50.00 (1.47)	3,731.70 (1.96)	3,731.70 (1.89)
4. Live stock	7,379.74 (6.30)	6,708.33 (2.38)	8,850.00 (1.15)	3,000.00 (0.18)	3,350.00 (98.53)	7,109.20 (3.73)	7,089.20 (3.58)
5. Others	—	—	—	—	—	—	—
Total:	1,17,015.24 (100.00)	2,81,475.00 (100.00)	7,70,700.00 (100.00)	17,26,400.00 (100.00)	3,400.00 (100.00)	1,90,540.20 (100.00)	1,98,028.40 (100.00)

Table 3.38

Per holding of farm family assets: for different size groups in developed area of underdeveloped district (Haveli Block - Poonch District) (in rupees)

Items	*Marginal farmers*	*Small farmers*	*Medium farmers*	*Large farmers*	*Landless labourers*	*All farmers on an combined average inclu-ding landless labourers*	*All farmers on an combined average exclu-ding landless labourers for land and farm building*
1. Land	50047.87 (81.97)	—	—	—	—	47045.00 (81.09)	50047.87 (82.01)
2. Farm building	47.85 (.08)	—	—	—	—	45.00 (.08)	47.87 (.08)
3. Implements & machinery	2236.50 (.78)	—	—	—	—	447.30 (.77)	447.30 (.77)
4. Live stock	10485.11 (17.17)	—	—	—	10,100 (96.81)	10462.00 (18.03)	10462.00 (17.15)
5. Others	—	—	—	—	333.33 (3.19)	20.00 (.03)	20.00 (.0.03)
Total:	61056.70 (100.00)	—	—	—	10433.33 (100.00)	58019.30 (100.00)	61025.04 (100.00)

Table 3.39

Per holding of farm family assets for different size holdings in underdeveloped area of under-developed district (Mendhar Block—Poonch District) (in rupees)

Items	*Marginal farmers*	*Small farmers*	*Medium farmers*	*Large farmers*	*Landless labourers*	*All farmers on an combined average including landless labourers*	*All farmers on an combined average excluding landless labourers for land and farm building only*
1. Land	78285.71 (88.08)	260133.33 (92.99)	433466.67 (91.77)	—	—	107376.00 (89.15)	111850.00 (89.53)
2. Farm building	158.33 (0.18)	383.33 (0.14)	283.33 (0.06)	—	—	173.00 (0.14)	180.21 (0.15)
3. Implements & machinery	198.81 (0.22)	233.33 (0.08)	6916.67 (1.46)	—	125.00 (0.75)	601.00 (0.50)	601.00 (0.48)
4. Live stock	10236.19 (11.52)	19000.00 (6.79)	31666.67 (6.71)	—	16470.00 (99.25)	12297.20 (10.21)	12297.20 (9.84)
5. Others	—	—	—	—	—	—	—
Total:	88879.04 (100.00)	279749.99 (100.00)	472333.34 (100.00)	—	16595.00 (100.00)	120447.20 (100.00)	124928.41 (100.00)

the major asset which accounts for about 95% of the total assets covered under survey. The second important asset of marginal farmers, small farmers and medium farmers is livestock. Whereas livestock is the main asset for landless labourers, implements and machinery are the important assets of large farmers.

Family Income

Income reflects the overall financial position of a farmer and his capacity for repayment of loans. Family income is derived from different sources. A farmer has income from: farm produce, dairying, hiring of implements, trade and commerce, service and others.

Table 3.40 reveals that the total income of 200 beneficiaries has been estimated at Rs.22,27,252 p.a. This gives yearly per family average of Rs.11,136. On this basis per capita income has been computed at Rs.1736 per annum.

Table 3.40 further reveals that out of total income of Rs.22,27,252, 38.85 per cent is derived from farm produce, followed by services (18.58%), other miscellaneous sources (16.61%), dairying (13.07%) and trade and commerce with 4.02%.

Table 3.40

Per Annum Total Income from all sources of all the farmers covered under survey in Jammu Division (in rupees)

Sources of Income	*Total Income*	*%age of total income*
1. Farm Income	8,66,116	38.88
2. Dairying	2,91,056	13.07
3. Hiring of Implements	1,96,840	8.84
4. Trade & Commerce	89,500	4.02
5. Service	4,13,820	18.58
6. Others	3,69,920	16.61
Total:	22,27,252	100.00

Family Income in Blocks

The distribution of population according to their sources of income as given in table 3.41 to 3.44 reveals that farm income constitutes the major source of income of the population covered under survey.

Total average income of a farmer in R.S. Pura block and in Dansal block of Jammu district has been worked out at Rs.21190.24 and Rs.9439.30 respectively. Conversely, in Haveli block and in Mendhar block of Poonch district, average annual income is only Rs.3991.20 and Rs.9924.30 respectively. The main source of income in R.S. Pura block is the farm income which constitutes 53.13 per cent of the total income, whereas in other blocks of Jammu Division, non-farm income is the major source of income. Non-farm income consists of income from dairying, hiring of implements, trade and commerce, services and other miscellaneous sources. Farm income of Dansal block constitutes about 19.17 per cent of the total income, in Haveli block 32.32 per cent and in Mendhar block 29.29 per cent.

Large farmers of R.S. Pura Block derive 60.30% of their incomes from farming, the corresponding income (52.76%) in Dansal block obtained from hiring of implements etc. Medium farmers of R.S. Pura block have farm income (52.84 per cent) as a major source of income but in Dansal block their main source of earning is jobs in Govt. and private sectors (75.36%). In Mendhar block, Dairying is the major source of income accounting for 32.20% of the total income of medium farmers. Small farmers of R.S. Pura block have farm income (38%) as a main source of income whereas small farmers of Dansal block and Haveli block have service as the main source of income which has been computed at 52.47 per cent and 73.33 per cent respectively.

Marginal farmers of R.S. Pura block have farm income as a major source of income which constitutes about 44.65 per cent of their total income. The marginal farmers of Dansal block, Haveli block and Mendhar blocks, have miscellaneous sources of income as a major source.

The position of landless labourers in all the four blocks is practically same; they are almost dependent on miscellaneous sources of income which ranges between 43 per cent to 100 per cent of their total incomes.

Table 3.41

Per family per annum Income according to classification of people in developed area of developed district (R.S. Pura Block—Jammu District)

(in Rupees)

Classification	*Farm Income*	*Non-Farm Income*					*Total Income*
		Diarying	*Hiring of Implements*	*Trade & Commerce*	*Service*	*Others*	
Marginal Farmers	3208.58 (44.65)	733.68 (10.21)	—	742.11 (10.33)	1326.32 (18.46)	1174.74 (16.35)	7185.43 (100.00)
Small Farmers	6672.38 (38.00)	3574.13 (20.36)	—	1500 (8.54)	1912.50 (10.89)	3900.00 (22.21)	17559.01 (100.00)
Medium Farmers	11726.00 (52.24)	2900.00 (12.92)	6620.00 (29.49)	—	—	1200.00 (5.35)	22446.00 (100.00)
Large Farmers	26570.31 (60.30)	1452.50 (3.30)	10087.50 (22.00)	1475.00 (3.35)	3275.00 (7.43)	1200.00 (2.72)	44060.31 (100.00)
Landless Farmers	—	540.00 (8.46)	—	720.00 (11.29)	1680.00 (26.33)	3440.00 (53.92)	6380.00 (100.00)
Total Average Income:	11258.38 (53.13)	1500.66 (7.08)	3492.80 (16.48)	1066.00 (5.03)	2026.00 (9.56)	1846.40 (8.72)	21190.24 (100.00)

Table 3.42

Per Family Per Annum Income according to classification of people in underdeveloped area of Developed district (Dansal Block—Jammu District).

(in Rupees)

Classification	*Farm Income*	*Non-Farm Income*					*Total Average Income*
		Dairying	*Hiring of Implements*	*Trade & Commerce*	*Service*	*Others*	
Marginal Farmers	1330.64 (17.44)	557.64 (7.37)	—	902.56	2044.10 (26.79)	2794.87 (36.63)	7629.81 (100.00)
Small Farmers	3752.17 (28.53)	300.00 (2.58)	1366.67 (10.39)	166.67	6900.00 (52.47)	66.67 (5.07)	13152.18 (100.00)
Medium Farmers	4777.50 (18.75)	1500.00 (5.89)	—	—	19200.00 (75.36)	—	25477.00 (100.00)
Large Farmers	6534.00 (24.63)	—	14000.00 (52.76)	—	—	600.00 (22.61)	26534.00 (100.00)
Landless Labourers	—	—	—	—	4500 (50.00)	4500 (50.00)	9000.00 (100.00)
Total average income	1809.94 (19.17)	530.96 (5.63)	444.00 (4.70)	724.00 (7.67)	3370.40 (35.71)	2580 (27.12)	9439.30 (100.00)

Table 3.43

Per Family Pér Annum Income according to classification of people in Developed Area of Under-developed district (Haveli Block—Poonch District)

(in Rupees)

Classification	*Farm Income*	*Non-Farm Income*					*Total Income*
		Diarying	*Hiring of Implements*	*Trade & Commerce*	*Service*	*Others*	
Marginal Farmers	1368.09 (33.96)	986.38 (24.68)	—	—	—	1674.47 (41.56)	4028.94 (100.00)
Small Farmers	—	—	—	—	—	—	—
Medium Farmers	—	—	—	—	—	—	—
Large Farmers	—	—	—	—	—	—	—
Landless Labourers	—	866.67 (25.49)	—	—	—	2533.33 (74.50)	3400.00 (100.00)
Total average income	1286.00 (32.22)	979.20 (24.53)	—	—	—	1726.00 (43.25)	3991.20 (100.00)

Table 3.44

Per Family Per Annum Income according to classification of people in Under-developed area of Under-developed district (Mendhar Block—Poonch District)

(in rupees)

Classification	*Farm Income*	*Non-Farm Income*					*Total Income*
		Dairying	*Hiring of Implements*	*Trade & Commerce*	*Service*	*Others*	
Marginal Farmers	2509.52	2702.74	—	—	238.10	1159.52	6609.88
	(37.97)	(40.89)			(3.60)	(17.54)	(100.00)
Small Farmers	10666.67	2666.66	—	—	36666.67	—	50,000.00
	(21.33)	(5.32)			(73.33)		(100.00)
Medium Farmers	3666.67	6333.33	—	—	8000.00	1666.67	19,666.67
	(18.64)	(32.20)			(40.68)	(8.48)	(100.00)
Large Farmers	—	—	—	—	—	—	—
Landless Labourers	—	—	—	—	—	4800.00	4800.00
						(100.00)	(100.00)
Total Average Income	2968.00 (29.10)	2810.30 (28.32)	—	—	2880.00 (29.02)	1266.00 (12.76)	9924.30 (100.00)

There is intimate relationship between the characteristics of the beneficiaries and the finances obtained by them. Finances depend on their need and the capacity to repay the loans. The needs of the farmers are determined by the size of holdings and land use pattern. The capacity to repay is based on the basis of economic status and the size of holdings of the farmers.

4
SOURCES OF FINANCE

The present chapter is based on field survey conducted by the researcher. It discusses in detail the sources of finance, the relative importance of each of these sources in financing agriculture and the outstandings of the beneficiaries on the date of survey.

Following are the different sources of agricultural finance:

(i) Commercial Banks,

(ii)* Regional Rural Banks,

(iii) Central Co-operative Land Development Banks, and

(iv) Co-operative Societies and Co-operative Banks.

These sources were identified during the course of the survey conducted.

Distribution of Finances according to Sources

Block-wise distribution of finance according to financial institutions is given in Table 4.1. The table under reference shows that the commercial banks account for the maximum contribution of 47.06 per cent to the total agricultural finance. The other institutions in order of importance and Central Co-operative Land Development Bank (29.15%), Regional Rural Bank (16.38%) and Co-operative Banks and Societies (7.41%).

---

* For study purposes Regional Rural Banks have been separated from the commercial banks because of its own importance in the rural economy of the State.

The analysis of different agencies in different blocks shows that the commercial banks played a dominant role in financing agricultural operations in R.S. Pura block. Its contribution to this block has been estimated at 50.75 per cent of the total finances supplied to all the four blocks under study. Other blocks in order of importance are Haveli block of Poonch tehsil (22.28%), Mendhar block of Mendhar tehsil (14.01%) and Dansal block of Jammu tehsil (12.96%). The table further shows that the commercial banks in these blocks have supplied finance to the tune of Rs. 3970 per family and Rs. 619 per capita to finance their agricultural operations. As against this average of Rs. 3970 per family, the actual finances varied between the minimum of Rs. 2058 in Dansal block and maximum of Rs. 8059 in R.S. Pura block. The table under reference further shows that the contribution per family of commercial banks, have been worked out at Rs. 3538 in Haveli block and Rs. 2224 in Mendhar block.

It is interesting to point out that as against the average, the per family finance of Rs. 3970, the actual finance per family in each of these blocks except R.S. Pura, is lower than the average. It is only in R.S. Pura block, the actual contribution is much higher than the average.

Like-wise, the contribution of the Regional Rural Banks to all the four blocks as given in table 4.1 varies between the minimum of 18.46 per cent in Mendhar block and the maximum of 30.61 per cent in Haveli block. The proportion of the remaining two blocks, i.e., R.S. Pura and Dansal has been worked out at 23.41 per cent and 27.34 per cent respectively. The contribution per family and per capita finance may be obtained from the table under reference.

Central Co-operative Land Development Banks have also contributed about 29 per cent of the total finances for agricultural development. Its activities have been confined only to the two out of four blocks covered under study. These blocks are R.S. Pura and Dansal of Jammu district. The study shows that the R.S. Pura block accounted for the maximum proportion of 83.49 per cent and the Dansal block, the remaining 16.51 per cent. Per family and per capita contribution may be obtained from the table under reference.

Co-operative banks and societies are also contributing towards agricultural development. Their influence is much actively felt in the Mendhar block of Poonch District and R.S. Pura block of Jammu District. Mendhar block accounted for about 41 per cent of the total finances and

Table 4.1

Distribution of Finance by Financial Institutions in Jammu Division

(in Rupees)

Area covered under survey	*Commercial Banks*				*Regional Rural Banks*			
	Total	*%age*	*Per family*	*Per capita*	*Total*	*%age*	*Per family*	*Per capita*
1. R.S. Pura Block of R.S. Pura Tehsil (District Jammu)	4,02,950	50.75	8059	1232.26	64,700	23.41	1294	197.86
2. Dansal Block of Jammu Tehsil (District Jammu)	1,02,910	12.96	2058	316.65	75,553	27.34	1511	232.47
3. Haveli Block of Poonch Tehsil (District Poonch)	1,76,900	22.28	3538	672.62	84,600	30.61	1692	321.29
4. Mendhar Block of Mendhar Tehsil (District Poonch)	1,11,200	14.01	2224	302.17	51,500	18.64	1030	139.95
Total:	7,93,960 (47.06)	100.00	3970	618.93	2,76,353 (16.38)	100.00	1381.77	215.40

(Contd.)

Co-operative Land Development				Co-operative Banks and Societies				Total			
Total	%age	Per family	Per capita	Total	%age	Per family	Per capita	Total	%age	Per family	Per capita
4,10,600	83.49	8212	1255.66	48,785	39.03	976	149.19	9,27,035	54.95	18541	2835
81,200	16.51	1624	249.85	8,400	6.72	168	025.85	2,68,063	15.89	5361	0825
—	—	—	—	17,000	13.60	340	64.64	2,78,500	16.51	5570	1059
—	—	—	—	50,800	40.65	1016	138.04	2,13,500	12.65	4270	580
4,91,800 (29.15)	100.00	2459	383.32	1,24,985 (7.41)	100.00	625	97.42	16,87,098 (100.00)	100.00	8436	1315

R.S. Pura block about 39 per cent. The shares of Haveli block and Dansal block have been worked out at 13.60 per cent and 6.72 per cent respectively.

The above discussion reveals that the maximum proportion of agricultural finance distributed in Jammu division flowed to R.S. Pura block to the tune of 54.95 per cent. It is followed by the Haveli block (16.51%), Dansal block (15.89%) and Mendhar block (12.65%). This disparity in distribution of loans is due to less avenues of heavy investments in agricultural operations of hilly area blocks, e.g., heavy machinery is not in use in the hilly area blocks (Dansal, Haveli and Mendhar) and loans for this purpose can not be obtained in these areas, hence the shares in obtaining loans from financial institutions in the other three blocks (hilly) of Jammu division is less.

Distribution of Finance by Commercial Banks in Jammu Division

Distribution of finance by the commercial banks to different groups of agriculturists according to their holdings is presented in Table 4.2. The table under reference indicates that large farmers account for the maximum of 46.6% of the total agricultural finance distributed by commercial banks. The other beneficiaries in order of importance are marginal farmers (43.35%), landless labourers (4.77%), small farmers (4.27%) and medium farmers (1.01%).

The analysis of block-wise distribution of agricultural finance by commercial banks to different size groups shows that large farmers of R.S. Pura block have managed to borrow the maximum proportion of agricultural finance to the tune of 91.82% of the total agricultural finance distributed in this block. However, the marginal farmers of Haveli block, Mendhar block and Dansal block have managed to get the maximum proportion of 91.41%, 83.81% and 71.53% of the total agricultural finance respectively. The reason being about 85% of the total population in these blocks is the population of marginal farmers.

The table under reference further shows that per capita finance by commercial banks has been estimated at Rs. 619. As against this average of Rs. 619, the actual finance (per capita) varied between the minimum of Rs. 148.15 in case of medium farmers and the maximum of Rs. 2846.15 in case of large farmers. In addition, the per capita contribution of commercial banks to landless labourers, marginal farmers and small

Table 4.2

Distribution of Finance by Commercial Banks in Jammu Division

(In Rupees)

Size Groups	R.S. Pura Block			Dansal Block			Haveli Block			Mendhar Block			Jammu Division		
	Total	%age to total	Per capita	Total	%age to total	Per capita	Total	%age to total	Per capita	Total	%age to total	Per capita	Total	%age to total	Per capita
1. Marginal farmers	15,650	3.88	146.26	73,610	71.53	287.54	1,61,700	91.41	649.40	93,200	83.81	303.58	3,44,160	43.25	374.49
2. Small farmers	10,400	2.58	221.28	23,500	22.84	671.43	—	—	—	—	—	—	33,900	4.27	316.82
3. Medium farmers	—	—	—	—	—	—	—	—	—	8,000	7.19	400.00	8,000	1.01	148.15
4. Large farmers	3,70,000	91.82	2936.51	—	—	—	—	—	—	—	—	—	3,70,000	46.60	2846.15
5. Landless labourers	6,900	1.72	222.50	5,800	5.63	483.33	15,200	8.59	1085.71	10,000	9.00	625.00	37,900	4.77	519.18
Total:	4,02,950	100.00	1232.26	1,02,910	100.00	316.65	1,76,900	100.00	672.62	1,11,200	100.00	302.17	7,93,960	100.00	618.83

farmers has been estimated at Rs. 519.18, Rs. 374.49 and Rs. 316.82 respectively.

Per capita finance in case of marginal farmers (Rs. 649.40) is the highest in Haveli block as compared to their counterparts in other blocks covered under survey. Similarly, the per capita finance in case of small farmers of Dansal block (Rs. 671.43) and landless labourers of Haveli block (Rs. 1085.71) is the highest as compared to other beneficiaries in other blocks. The per capita borrowing of medium farmers of Mendhar block and large farmers of R.S. Pura block has been estimated at Rs. 400 and Rs. 2938.51 as against their average per capita of Rs. 148.15 and Rs. 2846.15 respectively. It is also observed that small farmers from Haveli block and Mendhar block, medium farmers from R.S. Pura block, Dansal block and Haveli block, large farmers from Dansal block, Haveli block and Mendhar block have not borrowed any amount from the commercial banks.

Distribution of Agricultural Finance by Regional Rural Banks in Jammu Division

Regional rural banks have sanctioned the highest proportion of agricultural finance to marginal farmers of Jammu division to the tune of 89.99 per cent. They are followed by landless labourers (10.27%), small farmers (3.62%), medium farmers (1.52%) and large farmers (1.48%).

An critical examination of table 4.3 reveals that the marginal farmers in all the four blocks covered under survey, have borrowed the maximum proportion of agricultural finance as compared to other categories of beneficiaries. The respective percentage in borrowings by the marginal farmers from Regional Rural Banks in different blocks has been worked out at 51.78% in R.S. Pura block, 97.35% in Dansal block and 100% in each of the Haveli and Mendhar blocks. The proportion of borrowings by the small farmers in R.S. Pura block is worked out at 12.36% which is higher than that of their counterparts in Mendhar block. Other category of beneficiaries who have borrowed from the Regional Rural Banks and medium farmers (6.49%), large farmers (6.34%) and landless labourers (23.03%) of R.S. Pura block only.

The table under reference further reveals that Haveli block accounts for the highest per capita financing of Rs. 321.67 by Regional Rural Banks. Other blocks in order of importance are Dansal Block

Table 4.3

Distribution of Finance by Regional Rural Banks in Jammu Division

Size Groups	*R.S. Pura Block*			*Dansal Block*			*Haveli Block*			*Mendhar Block*			*Jammu Division*		
	Total	*%age to total*	*Per capita*	*Total*	*%age to total*	*Per capita*	*Total*	*%age to total*	*Per capita*	*Total*	*%age to total*	*Per capita*	*Total*	*%age to total*	*Per capita*
1. Marginal farmers	33,500	51.78	313.08	73,553	97.35	287.32	84,600	100.00	339.76	51,500	100.00	167.75	2,43,153	89.99	264.58
2. Small farmers	8,000	12.36	170.21	2,000	2.65	057.14	—	—	—	—	—	—	10,000	3.62	93.46
3. Medium farmers	4,200	6.49	262.50	—	—	—	—	—	—	—	—	—	4,200	1.52	77.48
4. Large farmers	4,100	6.34	032.54	—	—	—	—	—	—	—	—	—	4,100	1.48	31.54
5. Landless labourers	14,900	23.03	474.19	—	—	—	—	—	—	—	—	—	14,900	5.39	204.11
Total:	64,700	100.00	197.86	75,553	100.00	232.47	84,600	100.00	321.67	51,500	100.00	147.99	2,76,353	100.00	215.40

(Rs. 232.47), R.S. Pura block (Rs. 197.86) and Mendhar block (Rs. 147.99). Size-wise distribution of per capita financing by Regional Rural Banks shows that marginal farmers account for the maximum of Rs. 264.58, followed by landless labourers (Rs. 204.11), small farmers (Rs. 93.46), medium farmers (Rs. 77.78) and large farmers (Rs. 31.54). It is also observed from the table under reference that marginal farmers of Haveli block and small farmers of R.S. Pura block have got the highest per capita finance of Rs. 339.76 and Rs. 170.20 as compared to their counterparts in other blocks respectively. Other categories of beneficiaries are landless labourers, medium farmers and large farmers from R.S. Pura block only. Their respective per capita borrowings are Rs. 474.19, Rs. 262.50 and Rs. 32.54.

Distribution of Agricultural finance by Central Co-operative Land Development Banks in Jammu Division

Role of Central Co-operative Land Development Banks in financing the agricultural operations of different size groups is presented in table 4.4. The table under reference shows that out of the total agricultural finance distributed by Central Co-operative Land Development banks, large farmers have made more efforts to secure the maximum proportion to the tune of 85.03%. The proportion of marginal and small farmers is very low owing to their inability to go in for long-term and medium-term loans which are provided by this source for buying tractors and other durable agricultural assets related to agricultural operations.

Block-wise distribution of finance by Central Co-operative Land Development Banks to different size groups shows that it has played a very prominent role in financing the agricultural operations of large farmers in R.S. Pura block and in Dansal block of Jammu division. Its respective contribution in these two blocks has been estimated at 85.12 per cent and 84.61 per cent.

The table under reference further shows that the Central Co-operative Land Development Banks have supplied per capita finance of Rs. 383.32 on an average. As against this average of Rs. 383.32, the actual finances varied between the maximum of Rs. 1255.66 in R.S. Pura block and minimum of Rs. 249.85 in Dansal block. It is further observed that the per capita contribution of Central Co-operative Land Development Banks in Haveli and Mendhar blocks is nil.

It is interesting to point out that as against the average per capita financing of Rs. 383.32, the actual finance per capita among different

Table 4.4

Distribution of Finance by Central Co-operative Land Development Bank in Jammu Division

(In Rupees)

Size Groups	R.S. Pura Block			Dansal Block			Haveli Block			Mendhar Block			Jammu Division		
	Total	%age to total	Per capita	Total	%age to total	Per capita	Total	%age to total	Per capita	Total	%age to total	Per capita	Total	%age to total	Per capita
1. Marginal farmers	44,500	10.84	415.89	6,000	7.39	023.44	—	—	—	—	—	—	50,500	10.27	054.95
2. Small farmers	16,600	4.04	353.19	—	—	—	—	—	—	—	—	—	16,600	3.38	155.14
3. Medium farmers	—	—	—	6,500	8.00	361.11	—	—	—	—	—	—	6,50C	1.32	120.37
4. Large farmers	3,49,500	85.12	2773.81	68,700	84.61	171.75	—	—	—	—	—	—	4,18,200	85.03	3216.92
5. Landless labourers	—	—	—	—	—	—	—	—	—	—	—	—	—	—	—
Total:	4,10,600	100.00	1255.66	81,200	100.00	249.85	—	—	—	—	—	—	4,91,800	100.00	383.32

size groups except large farmers is lower than the average. It is only in case of large farmers, the actual contribution is much higher than the average. It is also observed that Central Co-operative Land Development Banks are not meant for landless labourers as no one from this category has got opportunity to borrow from this source.

Distribution of Agricultural Finance by Co-operative Banks and Societies in Jammu Division

Distribution of finance by Co-operative Banks and Societies to different size groups reveals that marginal farmers account for the maximum share of 48.70% of the total agricultural finance distributed by Co-operative Banks and Societies. The other beneficiaries in order of importance are large farmers (29.20%), small farmers (13.30%) and medium farmers (8.8%).

Block-wise examination of agricultural finance distributed by Co-operative banks and societies to different size groups shows that large farmers of R.S. Pura block have managed to borrow the maximum proportion of agricultural finance in this block to the tune of 74.82%. However, medium farmers of Dansal block (47.62%), marginal farmers of Haveli block (100%) and of Mendhar block (70.47%) have got the maximum proportions. Landless labourers of Jammu Division are found deprived from the benefits from this source as generally Co-operative banks and societies in rural area provide short-term loans for inputs purposes only which is not required by the landless labourers.

Table 4.5 further explains that per capita financing from the Co-operative Banks and societies is the lowest as compared to other sources, estimated at Rs. 97.42. As against this average, the borrowing' of large farmers, medium farmers and small farmers have been higher than the average; their respective amounts have been estimated at Rs. 280.77, Rs. 203.70 and Rs. 155.34. It is the only among the marginal farmers that their per capita borrowing has been estimated at Rs. 66.23 which is below the average.

Again large farmers from R.S. Pura block are found to manage the highest per capita finance of Rs. 289.68. Among medium farmers, small farmers and marginal farmers their per capita finance is the highest in Mendhar block which is estimated at Rs. 350, Rs. 320 and Rs. 116.61 respectively.

Table 4.5

Distribution of Finance by Co-operative Banks & Societies in Jammu Division.

(In Rupees)

Size Groups	R.S. Pura Block			Dansal Block			Haveli Block			Mendhar Block			Jammu Division		
	Total	%age to total	Per capita	Total	%age to total	Per capita	Total	%age to total	Per capita	Total	%age to total	Per capita	Total	%age to total	Per capita
1. Marginal farmers	6,065	12.43	56.68	2,000	23.81	7.81	17,000	100.00	68.27	35,800	70.47	116.61	60,865	48.70	66.23
2. Small farmers	6,220	12.75	132.34	2,400	28.57	68.57	—	—	—	8,000	15.75	320.00	16,620	13.30	155.33
3. Medium farmers	—	—	—	4,000	47.62	222.22	—	—	—	7,000	13.78	350.00	11,000	8.80	203.70
4. Large farmers	36,500	74.82	289.68	—	—	—	—	—	—	—	—	—	36,500	29.20	280.77
5. Landless labourers	—	—	—	—	—	—	—	—	—	—	—	—	—	—	—
Total:	48,785	100.00	149.19	8,400	100.00	25.85	17,000	100.00	64.64	50,800	100.00	138.04	1,24,985	100.00	97.42

Source-wise Distribution of Agricultural Finance to Different Size Groups of Farmers in Jammu Division

Survey reveals that out of the total distributed agricultural finance by all financial institutions in Jammu division, maximum proportion to the tune of 49.13% is received by the large farmers. Other categories of beneficiaries in order of importance are marginal farmers (41.4%), small farmers (4.57%), landless labourers (3.13%) and medium farmers (1.76%).

Analysis of different agencies in financing of different size groups indicates that the commercial banks has come forward in a big way in financing the agricultural operations of marginal farmers, small farmers and landless labourers. Their respective percentages of loans from commercial banks are estimated at 49.25%, 43.96% and 77.77%. It is further observed from table 4.6 that large farmers and medium farmers have borrowed the maximum proportion of finances from the Central Co-operative land development bank (30.46%) and Co-operative banks & Societies (37.03%) respectively.

The table under reference further shows that commercial banks have provided highest per capita finance of Rs. 618.84. Other institutions in order of importance are Central Co-operative Land Development Banks (Rs. 383.32), Regional Rural Banks (Rs. 215.40) and Co-operative Banks and Societies (Rs. 97.42). Among all the farmers covered under survey, large farmers account for the highest per capita finances of Rs. 6375.38; other categories in order of importance are marginal farmers (Rs. 760.26), landless labourers (Rs. 723.29), small farmers (Rs. 720.75) and medium farmers (Rs. 550). It is observed from the table under reference that marginal farmers, small farmers and landless labourers have got the maximum proportion of their total per capita borrowings from the commercial banks to the tune of Rs. 374.49, Rs. 316.82 and Rs. 519.18 respectively. Like-wise large farmers and medium farmers have obtained maximum proportion of their per capita financing from the Central Co-operative Land Development Banks (Rs. 3216.92) and Co-operative Banks and Societies (Rs. 203.70) respectively.

Block-wise Distribution of Agricultural Finance According to Sources and Beneficiaries

It has already been stated that four blocks have been taken up for making an indepth study. They are: (i) R.S. Pura, (ii) Dansal, (iii) Haveli and (iv) Mendhar.

Table 4.6

Source-wise Distribution of Agricultural Finance to Different Size Groups of Farmers in Jammu Division

(in Rupees)

Sources	Marginal farmers			Small farmers			Medium farmers			Large farmers			Landless labourers			Total		
	Total	%age to total	Per capita	Total	%age to total	Per capita	Total	%age to total	Per capita	Total	%age to total	Per capita	Total	%age to total	Per capita	Total	%age to total	Per capita
Commercial Banks	344160	49.25	374.49	33900	43.96	316.82	8000	26.94	148.15	370000	44.64	2846.15	37900	71.77	519.18	793960	47.07	618.84
Regional Rural Banks	243153	34.80	264.58	10000	12.96	93.46	4200	14.14	77.78	4100	0.49	31.54	14900	28.23	204.11	276353	16.38	215.40
Central Co-op Land Develop-ment Banks	50500	7.24	54.95	16600	21.52	155.14	6500	21.84	120.37	418200	50.46	3216.92	-	-	-	491800	29.15	383.32
Co-op Banks & Societies	60865	8.71	66.23	16620	21.56	155.33	11000	37.03	203.70	36500	4.46	280.77	-	-	-	124985	7.40	97.42
Total:	698678 (41.41)	100.00	760.26	77120 (4.57)	100.00	720.75	29700 (1.76)	100.00	550.00	828800 (49.13)	100.00	6375.38	52800 (3.13)	100.00	723.29	1687098 (100.00)	100.00	1314.96

R.S. Pura Block: Table 4.7 shows that the proportion of borrowings from commercial banks to the total in each class of cultivator except landless labourers decreases from large farmers to marginal farmers. This is a clear indication of the tendency among commercial banks to lend money mainly to credit worthy farmers. Proportion of borrowings from commercial banks in R.S. Pura block is calculated at 48.68%, 25.23% and 15.69% in case of large farmers, small farmers and marginal farmers respectively.

It is interesting to note that the variation in the proportion of borrowings from Regional Rural Banks to the total does not show any consistent trend from class to class of cultivators. However, it may be noted that the percentage of borrowings from Regional Rural Banks to the total is 100% among medium farmers, 68.35% among landless labourers, 33.60% among marginal farmers, 19.4% among small farmers and it is only 0.54% among big farmers. This shows that Regional Rural Banks are ready to accommodate to all classes of beneficiaries especially to landless labourers and marginal farmers of R.S. Pura block.

Medium farmers and landless labourers did not report any borrowings from Central Co-operative Land Development Banks and Co-operative Banks and Societies. However, the proportion of borrowings from Central Co-operative Land Development Banks to the total in other categories of farmers is more or less constant. The proportion of borrowings from Central Co-operative Land Development Banks by large farmers, marginal farmers and small farmers has been worked out at 46%, 45%, and 40% respectively.

As regard Co-operative Banks & Societies, it may be stated that the medium farmers have not borrowed from them at all. However, the proportion of borrowings from Co-operative Banks & Societies is 15.04% in case of small farmers, 6.08% in case of marginal farmer and 4.8% in case of large farmers.

The table under reference further shows that per capita financing by commercial banks, central co-operative land development banks and co-operative societies is the highest to large farmers as compared with other categories of beneficiaries in R.S. Pura block. The corresponding figures of per capita financing are calculated at Rs. 2936.51, Rs. 2773.81 and Rs. 289.68 respectively. On the other hand, per capita financing by these institutions to marginal farmers is the lowest, worked out at Rs. 146.26, Rs. 415.89 and Rs. 56.68 respectively.

Table 4.7

Source-wise Distribution of Agricultural Finance to Different Size Groups of Farmers in R.S. Pura Block (Developed Area of Developed District).

(In Rupees)

Sources	Marginal farmers			Small farmers			Medium farmers			Large farmers			Landless labourers			Total		
	Total	%age to total	Per capita	Total	%age to total	Per capita	Total	%age to total	Per capita	Total	%age to total	Per capita	Total	%age to total	Per capita	Total	%age to total	Per capita
Commercial Banks	15650	15.69	146.26	10400	25.23	221.28	—	—	—	370000	48.68	2936.51	6900	31.65	222.58	402950	43.46	1232.26
Regional Rural Banks	33500	33.60	313.08	8000	19.41	170.21	4200	100.00	262.50	4100	0.54	32.54	14900	68.35	480.65	64700	6.98	197.86
Central Co-op Land Development Banks	44500	44.63	415.89	16600	40.27	353.19	—	—	—	349500	45.98	2773.81	—	—	—	410600	44.30	1255.66
Co-op Banks & Societies	6065	6.08	56.68	6220	15.09	132.34	—	—	—	36500	4.80	289.68	—	—	—	48785	5.25	149.19
Total:	99715 (10.78)	100.00	931.92	41220 (4.45)	100.00	877.02	4200 (0.45)	100.00	262.50	760100 (81.99)	100.00	6032.54	21800 (2.35)	100.00	703.23	927035 (100.00)	100.00	2834.97

The foregoing further states that Central Co-operative Land Development Banks have played a very prominent role in providing agricultural credit in R.S. Pura block; the role played by Co-operative Banks & Societies is insignificant. However, Regional Rural Banks have played a crucial role in the rural economy of R.S. Pura block. It has not only lent money to large and medium farmers but also to the landless labourers and marginal farmers in a big way.

Dansal Block: Position of Dansal Block as shown in table 4.8, is somewhat different to R.S. Pura block in regard to the distribution of agricultural finance according to different sources. As against the proportion of agricultural finance received by the marginal farmers, small farmers, medium farmers, large farmers and landless labourers in R.S. Pura block to the tune of 10.76%, 4.45%, 0.45%, 81.99% and 2.35%, their proportion in Dansal block is worked out at 57.88%, 10.41%, 3.92%, 25.63% and 2.16% respectively.

Per capita financing in Dansal block is comparatively lower than that of in R.S. Pura block. In case of large farmers, the per capita financing in Dansal is much higher than that of R.S. Pura block. Per capita financing in case of other categories of beneficiaries is also different which may be obtained from the table under reference.

The proportionate borrowings of marginal farmers, small farmers and landless labourers from commercial banks have been worked out at 47.44%, 84.23% and 100% respectively. Whereas the proportionate borrowings from Regional Rural Banks are 47.4% in respect of marginal farmers and 7.17% in respect of small farmers. However, medium farmers and large farmers have not borrowed any amount from commercial banks and Regional Rural Banks. Their main source of borrowings is the Central Co-operative Land Development Bank from where they have borrowed to the tune of 61.9% and 100% respectively. Co-operative banks & societies have lent to the tune of 1.29%, 8.6% and 38.10% of the total borrowings to marginal farmers, small farmers and medium farmers respectively.

It is clear from the foregoing discussion that all financial agencies except Co-operative Banks and Societies have played a balanced role in financing the agricultural operations of Dansal block. Their proportionate lending ranges between 30.29% to 38.39%. Conversely the financing from the Co-operative Banks and Societies is 3.13% only which is the lowest.

Table 4.8

Source-wise Distribution of Agricultural Finance to Different Size Groups of Farmers to Different Size Groups in Dansal Block (Underdeveloped Area of Developed District).

(in Rupees)

Sources	Marginal farmers			Small farmers			Medium farmers			Large farmers			Landless labourers			Total		
	Total	%age to total	Per capita	Total	%age to total	Per capita	Total	%age to total	Per capita	Total	%age to total	Per capita	Total	%age to total	Per capita	Total	%age to total	Per capita
Commercial Banks	73610	47.44	287.54	23500	84.23	671.47	—	—	—	—	—	—	5800	100.00	483.33	102910	38.39	316.65
Regional Rural Banks	73553	47.40	287.32	2000	7.17	57.14	—	—	—	—	—	—	—	—	—	75553	28.19	232.47
Central Co-op Land Development Banks	6000	3.87	23.44	—	—	—	6500	61.90	361.11	68700	100.00	17175	—	—	—	81200	30.29	249.85
Co-op Banks & Societies	2000	1.29	7.81	2400	8.60	68.57	4000	38.10	222.22	—	—	—	—	—	—	8400	3.13	25.85
Total:	155163 (57.88)	100.00	606.11	27900 (10.41)	100.00	797.14	10500 (3.92)	100.00	583.33	68700 (25.63)	100.00	17175	5800 (2.10)	100.00	483.33	268063 (100.00)	100.00	824.81

The main reason for lowest disbursement by co-operative societies is that these agencies provide only short-term loans for financing inputs only

Haveli Block: Table 4.9 indicates that the proportionate borrowings from commercial banks of marginal farmers and landless labourers have been calculated at 61.41% and 100% respectively. On the other hand, the proportionate borrowings from Regional Rural Banks and Co-operative Banks and Societies are confined only to the marginal farmers to the tune of 32.13% and 6.46% respectively. The role of Central Co-operative Land Development Banks is practically obliviant in Haveli Block of Poonch district. The reason for oblivisance is that all the farmers are small and marginal farmers and hence they do need not to buy tractors or machinery for which finances are extended by the Central Co-operative Land Development Bank.

The available per capita borrowing in Haveli block has been worked out at Rs. 672.62 from Commercial Banks, Rs. 321.67 from Regional Rural Banks and Rs. 64.64 from Co-operative Banks & Societies. This makes the total per capita borrowing of Rs. 1058.94. The average borrowing is below the borrowing level of landless labourers which has been computed at Rs. 1085.71.

It may be stated that the role of commercial banks in financing the agricultural operations in Haveli block is quite significant, as maximum proportion to the tune of 63.52% is lent out by this source and the balance by the Regional Rural Banks and Co-operative Banks & Societies to the tune of 30.38% and 6.1% respectively.

Mendhar Block: Table 4.10 reveals that the proportional borrowings from Commercial Banks by the marginal farmers, medium farmers and landless labourers have been worked out at 51.64%, 53.3% and 100% respectively. The proportionate borrowings from other sources like Regional Rural Banks and Co-operative Banks & Societies have been worked out at 28.53% and 19.83% respectively in case of marginal farmers. Whereas 100% and 46.67% are obtained from Co-operative Banks & Societies by small farmers and medium farmers respectively, there is complete absence of borrowings on the part of large farmers as they did not exist in this block. Hence the role of Central Co-operative Land Development Banks is nil in financing the agricultural operation of Mendhar block. Since Central Co-operative Land Development Banks lend money for the purchase of tractors etc. which are not required in this

Table 4.9

Source-wise Distribution of Agricultural Finance to Farmers in Different Size Groups in Haveli Block (Developed Area of Under-Developed District)

(in Rupees)

Sources	Marginal farmers			Small farmers			Medium farmers			Large farmers			Landless labourers			Total		
	Total	%age to total	Per capita	Total	%age to total	Per capita	Total	%age to total	Per capita	Total	%age to total	Per capita	Total	%age to total	Per capita	Total	%age to total	Per capita
Commrcial Banks	161700	61.41	649.40	—	—	—	—	—	—	—	—	—	15200	100.00	1085.71	176900	63.52	672.62
Regional Rural Banks	84600	32.13	339.76	—	—	—	—	—	—	—	—	—	—	—	—	84600	30.38	321.67
Central Co-op Land Development Banks	—	—	—	—	—	—	—	—	—	—	—	—	—	—	—	—	—	—
Co-op Banks & Societies	1700	6.46	68.27	—	—	—	—	—	—	—	—	—	—	—	—	17000	6.10	64.64
Total:	263300	100.00	1057.43	—	—	—	—	—	—	—	—	—	15200	100.00	1085.71	278500	100.00	1058.94

block due to its hilly tract, no amount has been provided by this institution.

The above discussion shows that role of commercial banks is significant as the maximum proportion of 52.08% of the total finance has been provided by this institution. Other two sources are Regional Rural Bank and Co-operative Societies; their contribution has been worked out at 24.12% and 23.8% respectively.

Purposewise Distribution of Finance to Different Size Groups in Jammu Division

Table 4.11 gives purpose-wise classification of borrowings among the five groups of beneficiaries. The table under reference shows that all the beneficiaries covered under survey in Jammu Division have borrowed for the following four purposes:

(i) Inputs,

(ii) Machinery & Implements,

(iii) Farm Building Improvement and Investment, and

(iv) Live stock.

Inputs: Total amount sanctioned for this purpose to all the farmers covered under survey is amounted to Rs.1,37,585 which is only the 8% of the total amount disbursed in Jammu Division for agriculture.

The table under reference further shows that data on the proportion of borrowings for inputs does not show any consistent trend among the different classes. However, the proportion is higher among medium farmers (41.08) which is followed by small farmers (24.15), marginal farmers (9.47) and large farmers (4.90).

The average of per capita finance for input purposes is worked out at Rs.107.24 which is below the per capita borrowings of small farmers (Rs.174.02), medium farmers (Rs.225.93) and large farmers (Rs.312.31). Per capita finance for input purposes is higher in case of large farmers whereas their proportionate borrowings for this purpose is the lowest.

Machinery and Implements: Total amount sanctioned by all the institutions to all farmers covered under survey for this purpose is amounted to Rs. 8,40,360 i.e. 50% of the total amount sanctioned in Jammu Division. However, the proportion of borrowings for machinery and implements is lowest among all farmers (6.48) while large farmers have

Table 4.10

Source-wise Distribution of Finance to Farmers of Different Size Groups in Mendhar Block (Under-Developed Area of Under-Developed District).

(in Rupees)

Sources	Marginal farmers			Small farmers			Medium farmers			Large farmers			Landless labourers			Total		
	Total	%age to total	Per capita	Total	%age to total	Per capita	Total	%age to total	Per capita	Total	%age to total	Per capita	Total	%age to total	Per capita	Total	%age to total	Per capita
Commercial Banks	93200	51.64	303.58	—	—	—	8000	53.33	400.00	—	—	—	10000	100.00	625.00	111200	52.08	302.17
Regional Rural Banks	51500	28.53	167.75	—	—	—	—	—	—	—	—	—	—	—	—	51500	24.12	139.95
Central Co-op Land Development Banks	—	—	—	—	—	—	—	—	—	—	—	—	—	—	—	—	—	—
Co-op Banks & Societies	35800	19.83	116.61	8000	100.00	320.00	7000	46.67	350.00	—	—	—	—	—	—	50800	23.80	138.04
Total:	180500	100.00	587.95	8000	100.00	320.00	15000	100.00	750.00	—	—	—	10000	100.00	625.00	213500	100.00	580.16

reported a higher proportion of borrowings (93.17) for this purpose. Medium farmers have not borrowed for this purpose at all. Marginal farmers shows a higher proportion of borrowings (9.33) for this purpose than to small farmers. This is natural as resources of marginal farmers to finance machinery and implements are limited. It may be noted that purposes grouped under machinery and implements are purchase of tractors, threshers, pumpsets, electric motors, power tillers and small agricultural implements. Borrowings for purchase of tractors have been reported only by large farmers. It is the more substantial farmers who invests in pumpsets and threshers.

The table under reference further shows that per capita finance of Rs. 5940 is the highest in case of large farmers whereas marginal farmers have got per capita finance of Rs. 70.90 and Rs. 46.73 which are below the average of Rs. 656.55.

Farm Building, Improvement and Investment: Farm building etc. accounts for the lowest proportion of 6% allocated in Jammu Division, which is amounted to Rs. 1,02,250 to all the farmers covered under survey. However, the importance of farm building, improvement and investment as a purpose of borrowings is universal, its relative importance varies from class to class. The relative importance of this purpose is lowest among large farmers (0.84) than any other classes because in comparison with other classes they borrow less for farm building, improvement and investments and limit their borrowings for machinery and implements. However, it is also clear from the table that the relative importance of borrowings for this purpose is higher among small cultivators (42.01).

The average of per capita finance for this purpose is worked out at Rs. 79.69 which is the lowest of all the heads. However, per capita finance for this purpose is higher and above the average among small farmers (Rs. 302.80) and medium farmers (Rs. 120.37) whereas per capita finance for this purpose is lowest in case of marginal farmers (Rs. 57.07), large farmers (Rs. 53.85) and landless labourers (Rs. 53.43).

It is surprising to note that landless labourers have no farm but even they have borrowed for farm building. It is because of the fact that they own farm equipments, etc. for labour work on farms for which they borrow.

Table 4.11

Purpose-wise Distribution of Finance to Farmers of Different Size Groups in Jammu Division.

(in Rupees)

Sources	Marginal farmers			Small farmers			Medium farmers			Large farmers			Landless labourers			Total		
	Total	%age to total	Per capita	Total	%age to total	Per capita	Total	%age to total	Per capita	Total	%age to total	Per capita	Total	%age to total	Per capita	Total	%age to total	Per capita
Inputs	66165	9.47	72.00	18620	24.15	174.02	12200	41.08	225.93	40600	4.90	312.31	—	—	—	137585	8.16	107.24
Machinery & Implements	65160	9.33	70.90	5000	6.48	46.73	—	—	—	772200	93.17	5940.00	—	—	—	842360	49.93	656.55
Farm building Improvement & Investment	52450	7.50	57.07	32400	42.01	302.80	6500	21.88	120.37	7000	0.84	53.85	3900	7.39	53.43	102250	6.06	79.69
Live Stock	514903	73.70	560.29	21100	27.36	197.20	11000	37.04	203.70	9000	1.09	69.23	48900	92.61	669.86	604903	35.85	471.48
Total:	698678	100.00	760.26	77120	100.00	720.75	29700	100.00	550.00	828800	100.00	6375.39	52800	100.00	723.29	1687098	100.00	1314.96

Live stock: It is an allied activity for which the institutions have financed to the tune of Rs. 6,04,903 i.e. 36% of the total amount sanctioned in Jammu Division. Table 4.11 shows that the proportion of borrowings of landless labourers in this regard is the highest to the tune of 92.63% of the total amount lent by these institutions. In case of large farmers it is only 1%.

The table under reference further shows that the financial assistance obtained by the marginal farmers has largely been devoted to the purchase of live stock. This constitutes more than 73% of the total borrowings by marginal farmers.

Per capita borrowings for this purpose is also higher among landless labourers which is calculated at Rs. 669.86, followed by marginal farmers (Rs. 560.29), medium farmers (Rs. 203.70) and large farmers (Rs. 69.23).

The foregoing reveals that the machinery and implement accounts for the maximum proportionate borrowings of 49.93% to the total agricultural finance. The other purposes of borrowings in order of importance are live stock (35.85%). Inputs (8.16%) and farm building improvement and investment (6.06%). Likewise per capita borrowings for machinery and implements is also the highest which is estimated at Rs. 656.55 followed by live stock (Rs. 471.48), inputs (Rs. 107.24) and farm building improvement and investment (Rs. 79.69).

Purpose-wise Distribution of Finance to Different Size Groups in R.S. Pura Block

Table 4.12 presents purpose-wise distribution of the credit availed by sample farmers in R.S. Pura block.

Inputs

The table under reference shows that the medium farmers account for the maximum proportionate borrowings of 28.57% for this purpose. Other farmers in order of importance are small farmers (15.09%), marginal farmers (6.08%) and large farmers (5.34%). However, the per capita borrowings for this purpose is higher among large farmers (Rs. 322.22) and it is the lowest in case of marginal farmers (Rs. 56.68). Per capita borrowings for this purpose in case of small farmers and medium farmers is worked out at Rs. 132.34 and Rs. 75 respectively.

Table 4.12

Purpose Distribution of Finance to Farmers of Different Size Groups in R.S. Pura Block.

(in Rupees)

Sources	Marginal farmers			Small farmers			Medium farmers			Large farmers			Landless labourers			Total		
	Total	%age to total	Per capita	Total	%age to total	Per capita	Total	%age to total	Per capita	Total	%age to total	Per capita	Total	%age to total	Per capita	Total	%age to total	Per capita
Inputs	6065	6.08	56.68	6220	15.09	132.34	1200	28.57	75.00	40600	5.34	322.22	—	—	—	54085	5.84	165.40
Machinery & Implements	25000	25.07	233.64	—	—	—	—	—	—	703500	92.55	5583.33	—	—	—	728500	78.58	2227.83
Farm Building Improve-ment & Investment	16500	16.55	154.21	22400	54.34	476.60	—	—	—	7000	0.92	55.56	3900	17.89	125.81	49800	5.37	152.29
Live Stock	52150	52.30	487.38	12600	30.57	268.08	3000	71.43	187.50	9000	1.19	71.43	17900	82.11	577.41	94650	10.21	289.45
Total	99715	100.00	931.91	41220	100.00	877.02	4200	100.00	262.50	760100	100.00	6032.54	21800	100.00	703.22	927035	100.00	2834.97

Machinery and Implements

The proportionate borrowings for this purpose is higher among large farmers (92.55%) and lower in case of marginal farmers (25.07%). Small farmers and medium farmers of R.S. Pura block have not borrowed any amount for this purpose at all. Per capita borrowings for this purpose is also the highest in respect of large farmers which is amounted to Rs. 5583.33 and the lowest in respect of marginal farmers to the tune of Rs. 233.64.

Farm Building, Improvement and Investment

The purchase of farm building, improvement and investment is more important for small farmers as the maximum proportion of borrowings (54.34%) for this purpose has been reported by them. Others in order of importance and landless labourers (17.89%), marginal farmers (16.55%) and large farmers (0.92%). Per capita borrowing for this purpose is also the highest among small farmers (Rs. 476.60) and it is the lowest among large farmers (Rs. 55.56). Medium farmers have not borrowed any amount for this purpose in R.S. Pura block.

Livestock

Here we may note that the need for live stock is universal. However, loans taken for this purpose vary from class to class of farmers. The proportionate borrowings for this purpose by the landless labourers is the highest to the tune of 82.11%. Other beneficiaries in order of importance are medium farmers (71.43%), marginal farmers (52.30%), small farmers (30.57%) and large farmers (1.19%). Again landless labourers are found to manage the highest per capita borrowings of Rs. 577.41. Among other categories of farmers, per capita borrowings for this purpose is worked out at Rs. 487.38 in case of marginal farmers, Rs. 268.08 in case of small farmers, Rs. 187.50 in case of medium farmers and Rs. 71.43 in case of large farmers.

Table under reference further shows that machinery and implements accounts the highest proportionate borrowings of 78.58%. Other purposes of borrowings in order of importance are live stock (10.21%), inputs (5.84%) and farm building improvement and investment (5.37%). The average of per capita borrowings has been worked out at Rs. 567.80, Rs. 73.77, Rs. 42.16 and Rs. 38.82 for the purchase of machinery and implement, live stock, inputs and farm building, improvement & investments respectively.

Purpose-wise Distribution of Finance to Different Size Groups in Dansal Block

Purpose-wise distribution of finance to different size groups of farmers is presented in table 4.13.

Inputs

The proportion of borrowings for inputs shows an increasing trend from marginal farmers to medium farmers which ranges between 4% to 38.10%. This is because the amount of inputs purchased by medium farmers would be higher than that by marginal ones. However, large farmers of Dansal block have not borrowed for this purpose, because of their own resources. Per capita borrowings for the purchase of inputs is also higher in respect of medium farmers (Rs. 222.22) and lower in respect of marginal farmers (Rs. 24.22).

Machinery and Implements: Table 4.13 further deals with data relating to the borrowings for machinery and implements among different groups of farmers. It may be noted that this purpose is important only in respect of large farmers, their proportionate borrowings for this purpose is 100%. Marginal farmers and small farmers have borrowed less for this purpose because of their small size of holdings. Their respective proportionate borrowings for this purpose has been worked at 16.22% and 17.92%. Per capita borrowings are the highest in case of large farmers to the tune of Rs.17,175 which is above the average of Rs.304.18. Per capita borrowings of other farmers have been calculated at Rs.98.28 and Rs.142.86 in case of marginal farmers and small farmers respectively.

Farm Building, Improvement & Investments: Borrowing for farm building, improvement and investment are insignificant among large farmers and landless labourers as nothing has been borrowed by them for this purpose. While other classes of farmers have reported proportionate borrowings for this purpose to the tune of 23.67%, 35.84% and 61.91% in respect of marginal farmers, small farmers and medium farmers respectively. Per capita borrowings for this purpose is also in increasing order from marginal farmers to medium farmers which are in between of Rs.140.43 in respect of marginal farmers and Rs.361.11 in respect of medium farmers.

Livestock: The proportionate borrowings for this purpose is the highest among landless labourers and marginal farmers which account for the maximum proportion of borrowings to the tune of 100% and 56.61%

Table 4.13

Purpose-wise Distribution of Finance to Farmers of Different Size Groups in Dansal Block.

(in Rupees)

Sources	Marginal farmers			Small farmers			Medium farmers			Large farmers			Landless labourers			Total		
	Total	%age to total	Per capita	Total	%age to total	Per capita	Total	%age to total	Per capita	Total	%age to total	Per capita	Total	%age to total	Per capita	Total	%age to total	Per capita
Inputs	6200	4.00	24.22	4400	15.77	125.71	4000	38.10	222.22	—	—	—	—	—	—	14600	5.45	44.92
Machinery & implements	25160	16.22	98.28	5000	17.92	142.86	—	—	—	68700	100.00	17175	—	—	—	98860	36.88	304.18
Farm building Improvement & Investment	35950	23.67	140.43	10000	35.84	285.71	6500	61.91	361.11	—	—	—	—	—	—	52450	19.57	161.38
Live Stock	87853	56.61	343.18	8500	30.47	24286	—	—	—	—	—	—	5800	100.00	483.33	102153	38.10	314.32
Total	155163	100.00	606.11	27900	100.00	797.14	10500	100.00	583.33	68700	100.00	17175	5800	100.00	483.33	268063	100.00	824.81

respectively. The proportionate borrowings in case of marginal farmers has been worked out at 30.47%. Medium and large farmers have reported no borrowings for this purpose. Per capita borrowings for this purpose is higher in case of landless labourers (483.33) because live stock is the main purpose of borrowings for them. Per capita borrowings have been calculated at Rs. 343.18 and Rs. 242.86 in case of marginal farmers and small farmers respectively.

It can be estimated from the foregoing discussion that in Dansal Block, live stock is the main purpose of borrowing which account for 38.10%. Other purposes of borrowings in order of importance are machinery & implements (36.88), farm building, improvement & investment (19.57) and inputs (5.45%). The average of per capita borrowings are also in the same order. It is maximum in case of live stock (Rs.79.62) and minimum in case of inputs (Rs.11.38).

Purpose-wise Distribution of Finance to Different Size Groups in Haveli Block

Table 4.14 sets out data on distribution of finance to different size groups according to the purposes in Haveli Block.

Inputs

According to the survey, in Haveli block there are only marginal farmers and landless labourers out of them, marginal farmers are entitled to get loans for this purpose. Their proportionate borrowings for this purpose has been worked out at 6.87 with per capita borrowings of Rs.72.69.

Machinery & Implements

As marginal farmers are the borrowers of this type of loans, hence their proportionate borrowings are the lowest to the tune of 4.56 with lowest per capita borrowing of Rs.48.19 because of their marginal size of holdings.

Farm Building, Improvement & Investment

Due to marginal size of holdings farmers of this block have not availed any such type of loans at all.

Table 4.14

Purpose-wise Distribution of Finance to Farmers of Different Size Groups in Haveli Block.

(in Rupees)

Sources	Marginal farmers			Small farmers			Medium farmers			Large farmers			Landless labourers			Total		
	Total	%age to total	Per capita	Total	%age to total	Per capita	Total	%age to total	Per capita	Total	%age to total	Per capita	Total	%age to total	Per capita	Total	%age to total	Per capita
Inputs	18100	6.87	—	—	—	—	—	—	—	—	—	—	—	—	—	18100	6.50	68.82
Machinery & Implements	12000	4.56	48.19	—	—	—	—	—	—	—	—	—	—	—	—	12000	4.31	45.63
Farm Building Improvement & Investments	—	—	—	—	—	—	—	—	—	—	—	—	—	—	—	—	—	—
Live stock	233200	88.57	936.55	—	—	—	—	—	—	—	—	—	15200	100.00	1085.71	248400	89.19	944.49
Total:	263300	100.00	1057.43	—	—	—	—	—	—	—	—	—	15200	100.00	1085.71	278500	100.00	1059.00

Live Stock

Live stock is the main purpose of borrowings of the people of Haveli block. The total borrowings of landless labourers have been worked out at 88.57% of their total borrowings. Out of the total per capita borrowings of Rs.1057.43 received by marginal farmers, Rs.936.55 has been utilised for this purpose. Whereas, the whole of per capita borrowings of landless labourers to the tune of Rs.1085.71 has been devoted to this purpose.

The table under reference further reveals that livestock is the main purpose of borrowings in Haveli block. 89.19% of the total disbursements in Haveli block have been utilised for the purchase of livestock. Other purpose of borrowings in Haveli block are inputs and machinery & implements which account for 6.50% and 4.31% respectively. Out of the total per capita borrowings of Rs.1059 in Haveli block, Rs.944.49 has been spent for the purchase of livestock, Rs.68.82 for inputs and Rs.45.63 for machinery & implements.

Purpose-wise Distribution of Finance to Different Size Groups in Mendhar Block

Table 4.15 presents data on borrowings according to purposes among different size groups.

Inputs

Whole of the borrowings of small farmers in Mendhar block is for this purpose. Whereas the proportionate borrowings of medium farmers and marginal farmers for this purpose has been worked out at 46.47 and 19.83 respectively. However, per capita borrowings of medium farmers for this purpose are higher than that the proportionate borrowings of small farmers. Large farmers did not exist in this block.

Machinery and Implements

Borrowings for machinery and implements have been made by marginal farmers to the tune of 1.66% of their total borrowings. Their per capita borrowing has been worked out at Rs.9.77.

Farm Building, Improvement & Investment

From Mendhar block, only the medium farmers have reported borrowings for this purpose to the tune of proportionate borrowings of 53.33 with per capita borrowings of Rs.400.

Table 4.15

Purpose-wise Distribution of Finance to Farmers of Different Size Groups in Mendhar Block.

(in Rupees)

Sources	Marginal farmers			Small farmers			Medium farmers			Large farmers			Landless labourers			Total		
	Total	%age to total	Per capita	Total	%age to total	Per capita	Total	%age to total	Per capita	Total	%age to total	Per capita	Total	%age to total	Per capita	Total	%age to total	Per capita
Inputs	35800	19.83	116.61	8000	100.00	320.00	7000	46.67	350.00	—	—	—	—	—	—	50800	23.79	138.04
Machinery & Implements	3000	1.66	9.77	—	—	—	—	—	—	—	—	—	—	—	—	3000	1.41	8.15
Farm building Improvement & Investments	—	—	—	—	—	—	8000	53.33	400.00	—	—	—	—	—	—	8000	3.75	21.73
Live stock	141700	78.51	461.56	—	—	—	—	—	—	—	—	—	10000	100.00	625.00	151700	71.05	412.23
Total:	180500	100.00	587.95	8000	100.00	320.00	15000	100.00	750.00	—	—	—	10000	100.00	625.00	213500	100.00	580.16

Livestock

It is the main purpose of borrowings for the landless labourers and for marginal farmers. Their respective proportionate borrowings for this purpose has been calculated at 100% and 78.51% with their per capita borrowings of Rs. 625 and Rs. 461.56 respectively.

It is also observed from the table 4.15 that 71.05% of the total borrowings in Mendhar block have been utilised for the purchase of live stock and the remaining 23.79%, 3.75% and 1.41% have been utilised for the purchase of inputs, farm building, improvement & investment and machinery and implements respectively.

Sources of Finance according to Purposes in Jammu Division

Table 4.16 gives the proportion of borrowings from different sources for specified purposes. It may be seen from the table under reference that the maximum proportion of financial assistance to the tune of 47.84% obtained from commercial banks has been devoted to the purchase of machinery and implements, a little less 45.94% for the purchase of live stock, 6.08% for farm building improvement and 0.14% for input.

On the other hand, financial assistance obtained from Regional Rural Banks has largely been devoted to the purchase of live stock. This constitutes more than 73% of the total borrowings. However, 12.64%, 9.95% and 4.18% of the total borrowings have been utilised for the purchase of machinery and implements, farm building improvements and inputs respectively.

Similarly, the maximum proportion of 86.87% of the total financial assistance obtained from Central Co-operative Land Development Bank has been spent on the purchase of machinery and implements, 7.74% for live stock and 5.39% for farm building improvement.

The entire financial assistance obtained from Co-operative Banks & Societies has been utilised for the purchase of inputs only.

The analysis of table 4.16 shows that commercial banks and Central Co-operative Land Development Banks are the best suited source of finance for the purchase of machinery & implements in Jammu Division. Whereas Regional Rural Banks is suited for the purchase of live stock and Co-operative Banks & Societies for the purchase of inputs.

The table under reference further shows that out of the total disbursements for agricultural operations in Jammu Division, maximum of

Table 4.16

Sources of Finance According to Purposes in Jammu Division (Area Covered Under Survey)

(in Rupees)

Purposes	*Amount advanced by Commercial Banks*		*Amount advanced by Regional Rural Banks*		*Amount advanced by Central Co-operative Land Development Banks*		*Amount advanced by Co-operative Banks & Societies*		*Total Advance*	
	Total	*%*	*Total*	*%*	*Total*	*%*	*Total*	*%*	*Total*	*%*
1. Inputs	1,100	0.14	11,500	4.18	—	—	1,24,985	100.00	1,37,585	8.16
2. Machinerty & Implements	3,80,360	47.84	34,800	12.64	4,27,200	86.87	—	—	8,42,360	49.93
3. Farm Building, Improvement & Investment	48,350	6.08	27,400	9.95	26,500	5.39	—	—	1,02,250	6.06
4. Live stock	3,65,250	45.94	2,01,553	73.23	38,100	7.74	—	—	6,04,903	35.85
Total:	7,95,060	100.00	2,75,253	100.00	4,91,800	100.00	1,24,985	100.00	16,87,098	100.00

49.93% has been utilised for the purchase of machinery and implements. It is followed by live stock (35.85%), inputs (8.16%) and farm building improvement and investments (6.06%).

Sources of Finance according to Purposes in R.S. Pura Block

Table 4.17 reveals that the maximum proportion of financial assistance obtained from commercial banks in R.S. Pura block has been utilised for the purchase of machinery and implements. This constitutes more than 91%. Other purposes of borrowings in order of importance are live stocks (4.36%) and farm building improvements (3.86%) whereas the financial assistance obtained from Regional Rural Banks have largely been devoted to the purchase of live stock (60.28%). The maximum proportion of 87.31% of the total financial assistance obtained from Central Co-operative Land Development Banks have been spent on the purchase of machinery and implements, remaining 9.28% on the purchase of live stock and 3.41% on farm building improvement etc.

Co-operative Banks & Societies is a source of agricultural finance for inputs as 100% of co-operative credit has been utilised for the purchase of inputs in R.S. Pura block.

Out of the total disbursements in R.S. Pura Block, maximum of which to the tune of 78.58% has been utilised for the purchase of machinery and implements whereas 10.71% for live stock, 5.84% for inputs and 5.37% for farm building improvements and investments.

Sources of Finance according to Purposes in Dansal Block

Table 4.18 indicates that out of the total financial assistance obtained from commercial banks in Dansal block, the maximum proportion of 57.91% has been devoted to the purchase of live stock, 20.02% to farm building improvement and 10.07% to machinery and implements.

The table under reference further shows that the maximum proportion of 56.32% of the total borrowings from Regional Rural Banks in Dansal block has been utilised for the purchase of live stock, followed by machinery and implements (26.21%), farm building improvement (9.26%) and inputs (8.21%). 84.61% of the borrowings from Central Co-operative Banks and Societies has been utilised for machinery and implements and the remaining of 15.39% for the purchase of farm building improvements. 100% of advances by Co-operative Banks and Societies have been utilised for the purchase of inputs.

Table 4.17

Source of Finance According to Purposes in R.S. Pura Block

(in Rupees)

Purposes	*Amount advanced by Commercial Banks*		*Amount advanced by Regional Rural Banks*		*Amount advanced by Central Co-operative Land Development Banks*		*Amount advanced by Co-operative Banks & Societies*		*Total Advance*	
	Total	*%*	*Total*	*%*	*Total*	*%*	*Total*	*%*	*Total*	*%*
1. Inputs	—	—	5,300	8.19	—	—	48,785	100.00	54,085	5.84
2. Machinery & Implements	3,70,000	91.82	—	—	3,58,500	87.31	—	—	7,28,500	78.58
3. Farm Building Improvement and Investments	15,400	03.82	20,400	31.53	14,000	3.41	—	—	49,800	5.37
4. Live Stock	17,550	4.36	39,000	60.28	38,100	9.28	—	—	94,650	10.21
Total:	4,02,950	100.00	64,700	100.00	4,10,600	100.00	48,785	100.00	9,27,035	100.00

Out of the total disbursements in Dansal block 38.10% have been used for the purchase of live stocks, followed by machinery and implements (36.88%), farm building improvement (19.57%) and inputs (5.45%).

Sources of Finance According to Purposes in Haveli Block

Table 4.19 represents the sources and purposes of borrowings in Haveli block. The entire financial assistance obtained from commercial banks has been devoted to the purchase of live stock and from Co-operative Banks and Societies to inputs. Whereas the maximum proportion of borrowings from Regional Rural Banks to the tune of 84.52% has been spent on live stock and only 1.30% for inputs and 4.18% on machinery and implements.

The table under reference further shows that 89.19% of the total disbursements in Haveli block has been spent on live stock, whereas 6.50% on inputs and only 4.31% on machinery and implements. Nothing has been borrowed for farm building improvements in this block, at the same time the role of Central Co-operative Land Development Bank is also found nil in providing loans to the farmers of Haveli Block.

Sources of Finance according to Purposes in Mendhar Block

The position of Mendhar block in this regard is the same as in Haveli block, i.e. 100% of the borrowings from commercial banks and co-operative societies have been spent on the purchase of live stock and inputs respectively. 99.17% of total borrowings from Regional Rural Banks has been also spent on the purchase of live stock and the balance of 5.83% on machinery and implements. Role of Central Co-operative Land Development Banks is also nil in this block and nothing has been borrowed for farm building improvement in this block from any sources.

Table 4.20 further reveals that 74.8% of the total disbursements in Mendhar block has been spent on live stock, 23.79% on inputs and 1.4% on machinery and implements.

In conclusion, it may be stated that the demand for agricultural finance in the developed block of Jammu Division is different from the demand of under developed blocks of Jammu Division. In R.S. Pura block, the demand for finance is more for machinery and implements (78.58%) as compared to other blocks where the demand is much for live stock. In Dansal block 38.1% of the total disbursements has been spent on live

Table 4.18

Sources of Finance According to Purposes in Dansal Block

(in Rupees)

Purposes	Amount advanced by Commercial Banks		Amount advanced by Regional Rural Banks		Amount advanced by Central Co-operative Land Development Banks		Amount advanced by Co-operative Banks & Societies		Total Advance	
	Total	%	Total	%	Total	%	Total	%	Total	%
1. Inputs	—	—	6,200	8.21	—	—	8,400	100.00	14,600	5.45
2. Machinery & Implements	10,360	10.07	19,800	26.21	68,700	84.61	—	—	98,860	36.88
3. Farm Building, Improvement & Investment	32,950	20.02	7,000	9.26	12,500	15.39	—	—	52,450	19.57
4. Live Stock	59,600	57.91	42,553	56.32	—	—	—	—	1,02,153	38.10
Total:	1,02,910	100.00	75,553	100.00	81,200	100.00	8,400	100.00	2,68,063	100.00

Table 4.19

Sources of Finance According to Purposes in Haveli Block

(in Rupees)

Purposes	Amount advanced by Commercial Banks		Amount advanced by Regional Rural Banks		Amount advanced by Central Co-operative Land Development Banks		Amount advanced by Co-operative Banks & Societies		Total Advance	
	Total	%	Total	%	Total	%	Total	%	Total	%
1. Inputs	—	—	1100	1.30	—	—	17,000	100.00	18,100	6.50
2. Machinery & Implements	—	—	12,000	4.18	—	—	—	—	12,000	4.31
3. Farm Building, Improvement & Investments	—	—	—	—	—	—	—	—	—	—
4. Live Stock	1,76,900	100.00	71,500	84.52	—	—	—	—	2,48,400	89.19
Total:	1,76,900	100.00	84,600	100.00	—	—	17,000	100.00	2,78,500	100.00

stock, in Haveli block 89.19% has been used for live stock and in Mendhar block 74.8% has been utilised for the purchase of live stock. Similarly the demand for agricultural finance differs from block to block. The main reason for this difference has been the extent of needs of the farmers living in the developed and under developed areas. Owing to better irrigation and other facilities in the developed area, the need for machinery and implements is more. In the under developed areas, need for purchase of live stock is much in order to supplement their incomes owing to non-availability of better irrigation and other facilities.

Extent of Outstanding in Jammu Division

In table 4.21, the percentage of outstanding liabilities against the total borrowings shows a significant variation among different classes of borrowers. The percentage of outstanding liability is much higher in case of small and medium farmers which has been worked out at 83.98% and 82.51% against the per family borrowings of Rs. 4536 and Rs. 4243 respectively. It means that small and medium farmers in Jammu division are also to clear their outstanding liabilities only by 35.91% and 37.99% including of interest liability to the tune of 19.89% and 20.50% respectively which is not a good indication. However, the outstanding liability in case of landless labourers and marginal farmers is comparatively low to the tune of 66.72% and 73.92% respectively, but their interest liability is not low in case of landless labourers even by making the highest repayment to the tune of 52.43% including interest liability of 19.15%. It is due to making repayments in longer durations.

The outstanding liability in case of big farmers is higher (76.26%) than that of landless labourers and marginal farmers but definitely lower than the outstanding liability of small and medium farmers. The interest liability is also lower to the tune of 15.65% but higher than that of the marginal farmers. Whereas their repayments are higher (39.39%) but lower than that of the landless labourers. It is all due to difference in time duration of repayments. Those, who are able to clear their outstanding liability within the limited period of time, their interest liability will be lower and those are not able to clear their outstanding liability within that period, they are bound to pay more interest. The reasons for not making repayment in time are given in the next chapter.

The table under reference further shows that on an average of all the farmers covered under survey, the outstanding liability has been

Table 4.20

Sources of Finance According to Purposes in Mendhar Block

(in Rupees)

Purposes	Amount advanced by Commercial Banks		Amount advanced by Regional Rural Banks		Amount advanced by Central Co-operative Land Development Banks		Amount advanced by Co-operative Banks & Societies		Total Advance	
	Total	*%*	*Total*	*%*	*Total*	*%*	*Total*	*%*	*Total*	*%*
1. Inputs	—	—	—	—	—	—	50,800	100.00	50,800	23.79
2. Machinery & Implements	—	—	3,000	5.83	—	—	—	—	3,000	1.41
3. Farm Building, Improvement & Investments	—	—	—	—	—	—	—	—	—	—
4. Live Stock	1,11,200	100.00	48,500	94.17	—	—	—	—	1,59,700	74.80
Total:	1,11,200	100.00	51,500	100.00	—	—	50,800	100.00	2,13,500	100.00

Table 4.21

Position of Outstanding in Jammu Division (Area Covered Under Survey) according to Size Groups.

(In Rupees)

Size Groups	*Advanced per family*		*Interest liabilities per family*		*Repayments per family*		*Outstanding per family*	
	Total	*%*	*Total*	*%*	*Total*	*%*	*Total*	*%*
Marginal Farmers	4,753	100.00	617.29	12.99	1,857	39.07	3513.29	73.92
Small Farmers	4,536	100.00	902.34	19.89	1,629	35.91	3809.34	83.98
Medium Farmers	4,243	100.00	870.06	20.50	1,612	37.99	3501.06	82.51
Large Farmers	48,753	100.00	7630.47	15.65	19,205	39.39	37178.47	76.26
Landless Farmers	4,400	100.00	842.63	19.15	2,307	52.43	2935.63	66.72
Average	8,435	100.00	1260.00	14.94	3,293.13	39.04	6402.37	75.90

worked out at 75.90% including of interest liability to the tune of 14.94%. It clearly indicates that the farmers of Jammu Division are able to clear their outstanding liability only to the tune of 39.04%, which is a serious problem. The solution of this problem is given in the last chapter of this thesis. Against per family borrowings of Rs.8435 in Jammu Division, their total repayments on an average has been worked out at Rs.3293 including the interest liability to the tune of Rs.1260 which left a net balance (outstanding) on an average per family to the tune of Rs.6402.37.

R.S. Pura Block

Table 4.22 indicates that per family outstanding liability in R.S. Pura block has been worked out at Rs.14267 which is nearly 77% of the per family borrowing of Rs.18541. The total repayments have been estimated at 39.47% including the interest liability of 16.42% of the total borrowings.

The table under reference further explains that outstanding liability in respect of medium farmers is the highest which has been estimated at 136%, including of interest liability to the tune of 36%. It means no repayments has been reported by the medium farmers in R.S. Pura block. The outstanding percentage in respect of marginal farmers has been worked out at 92.48% including the interest liability of 13.75%. It means marginal farmers of this block are able to clear their outstandings to the extent of 21.27% due to their depressed economic conditions.

Small farmers come next to marginal farmers in respect of outstanding liabilities, which have been worked out at 83% including interest liability to the tune of 13.73% in the per family borrowings of Rs.5153. Their repayment capacity has been worked out at 30.99% which is higher than the outstanding liability of marginal farmers. As regards large farmers and landless labourers, outstanding liability remains at the same level i.e. 74.30% and 75.89% respectively; however, their interest liability varies; it has been estimated at 16.69% in case of large farmers and 20.87% in case of landless labourers. Their repayments are also varying between 42% in case of large farmers and 45% in case of landless labourers.

The table under reference further reveals that interest liability in respect of medium farmers is the highest which has worked out at 36% as against 21% in case of landless labourers and 14% in case of both the marginal and small farmers. Repayments are higher in case of landless

Table 4.22

Position of Outstanding in R.S. Pura Block (Developed Area of Developed District) According to Size Groups.

(in Rupees)

Size Groups	Per family advanced		Per family interest liabilities		Per family repayment		Per family outstanding	
	Total	%	Total	%	Total	%	Total	%
Marginal Farmers	5248	100.00	721.46	13.75	1116	21.27	4854	92.48
Small Farmers	5153	100.00	707.54	13.73	1597	30.99	4263	82.73
Medium Farmers	2100	100.00	758.00	36.10	-	-	2858	136.10
Large Farmers	47506	100.00	7926.43	16.69	20134	42.38	35298	74.30
Landless Labourers	4360	100.00	910.10	20.87	1961	44.98	3309	75.89
Average	18541	100.00	3045.15	16.42	7319	39.47	14267	76.95

labourers (45%) as compared to 43% in case of large farmers, 31% in case of small farmers, 21% in case of marginal farmers and nothing in case of medium farmers.

Dansal Block

Table 4.23 discloses that outstanding liability in Dansal block is 76% of the total borrowings including interest liability to the tune of 15.68%. The actual per family borrowing has been estimated at Rs.5361 which is definitely lower than that of the R.S. Pura block in all respects. Total repayments including interest liability has been worked out at 39.57%.

Outstanding liability is higher in case of large farmers (98%) and lower in case of landless labourers (49%). Whereas interest liability in case of small farmers is higher (33%) and lower (4%) in case of large farmers. Repayments are higher in case of landless labourers (70%) and very low 6.30% in case of large farmers, because of the fact loans taken by large farmers are fresh loans.

Haveli Block

Table 4.24 describes that outstanding liability in Haveli block has been worked out at 74% including the interest liability to the tune of 7.16% against the per family borrowings of Rs.5570. It means that farmers of Haveli block are able to clear their outstanding liability including of interest to the extent of 33.13%.

The table under reference further shows that outstanding liability in respect of marginal farmers has been worked out at 74% as compared to 73% in case of landless labourers; their interest liability are 7% and 4% respectively. However, the repayments are 33% and 31% in respect of marginal farmers and landless labourers respectively.

Per family outstanding liability in Haveli block has been worked out at Rs.4123 against the loan of Rs.5570. It has repayed Rs.1845 including the interest charges of Rs.399.

Mendhar Block

Table 4.25 depicts the picture of Mendhar block regarding outstanding liabilities, repayments and interest liability of the borrowers covered under survey. The percentages in this respect has been worked out at 73%, 44% and 18% respectively.

Table 4.23

Position of Outstanding in Dansal Block (Under-Developed Area of Developed District) According to Size Groups.

(in Rupees)

Size Groups	*Advanced per family*		*Interest liabilities per family*		*Repayment per family*		*Outstanding per family*	
	Amount	*%*	*Amount*	*%*	*Amount*	*%*	*Amount*	*%*
Marginal Farmers	3979	100.00	697.46	17.52	2140	53.78	2536	63.74
Small Farmers	4650	100.00	1533.25	32.97	1671	35.94	4512	97.03
Medium Farmers	5250	100.00	787.21	14.99	1787	34.04	4250	80.95
Large Farmers	68700	100.00	2895.13	4.21	4334	6.30	67261	97.91
Landless Labourers	2900	100.00	580.00	20.03	2016	69.52	1415	48.79
Average	5361	100.00	840.64	15.68	2111	39.37	4092	76.32

Table under reference further shows that outstanding liability in respect of small farmers is the highest to the tune of 106% and lowest in case of landless labourers but their interest liability has been worked out at 38%. They have already paid about 104% of the actual borrowings. The excess payment has been the result of the default in repayments.

In conclusion, it can be said that outstanding liability in Jammu division is ranging between 73% to 77%. It is the lowest in case of Mendhar block and the highest in case of R.S. Pura block. It is very significant to point out that in the most developed block (R.S. Pura) of Jammu Division, outstanding liability is the highest (77%) as against the lowest (73%) in case of the most under developed block (Dansal). The interest liability is also ranging between 7% to 18%. Similarly repayments are ranging between 33% to 45%. It appears that farmers in the under developed area are more cautious and serious about repayment as compared to their counterparts in the developed areas.

Trend of Outstandings in Jammu Division

The total outstanding advances to all the two hundred families on the date of survey has been estimated at Rs.16,87,098. The liability of outstanding interest has been worked out at Rs.2,52,002 as per table 4.26, both make the total of Rs.19,39,100.

Total repayments on the date of survey has been estimated at Rs.6,58,625. This leaves a balance of Rs.12,80,475. The average total outstanding liability (principle and interest) per family has been estimated at Rs.6402.

Table 4.26 reveals that borrowings of the families covered under survey of R.S. Pura block have been estimated at Rs.9,27,035. On the date of survey; the outstanding interest has been estimated at Rs.1,52,257. This made a total liability of Rs.10,79,292. Repayments to the tune of Rs.3,65,933 have been made which left a balance of Rs.7,13,359. The average outstanding liability for farmers comes to Rs.14,268 given in table under reference.

The amount of outstanding borrowings of all the families in Dansal block has been worked out at Rs.2,04,553. This is much lower than the corresponding families in the R.S. Pura block (Developed area). The main reason for this low level of outstanding borrowings is the smaller magnitude of the borrowings taken by the agriculturists owing to limitation of their investments. Accordingly total outstanding interest has

Table 4.24

Position of Outstanding in Haveli Block (Developed Area of Under-Developed District) According to Size Groups

(in Rupees)

Size Groups	*Advance per family*		*Interest liabilities per family*		*Repayment per family*		*Outstanding per family*	
	Amount	*%*	*Amount*	*%*	*Amount*	*%*	*Amount*	*%*
Marginal Farmers	5602	100.00	411.23	7.34	1863	33.25	4150.86	74.09
Small Farmers	—	—	—	—	—	—	—	—
Medium Farmers	—	—	—	—	—	—	—	—
Large Farmers	—	—	—	—	—	—	—	—
Landless Labourers	5067	100.00	199.77	3.94	1577	31.12	3689.43	72.82
Average	5570	100.00	398.54	7.16	1845	33.13	4123.17	74.03

Table 4.25

Position of Outstanding in Mendhar Block (Under-Developed Area of Under-Developed District).

(in Rupees)

Size Groups	*Advanced per family*		*Interest liabilities per family*		*Repayment per family*		*Outstanding per family*	
	Amount	*%*	*Amount*	*%*	*Amount*	*%*	*Amount*	*%*
Marginal Farmers	4298	100.00	726.31	16.89	1923	44.75	3100.50	72.14
Small Farmers	2667	100.00	160.00	6.00	—	—	2827.00	106.00
Medium farmers	5000	100.00	1000.00	20.00	1238	24.76	4762.00	95.24
Large Farmers	—	—	—	—	—	—	—	—
Landless Labourers	5000	100.00	1900.00	38.00	5191	103.82	1709.00	34.18
Average	4270	100.00	755.70	17.70	1898	44.45	3128.08	73.25

been worked out at Rs.42,032. The total liability, therefore, comes to Rs. 3,10,095. They have made repayments to the tune of Rs. 1,05,592 which leaves the net outstanding liability of Rs.2,04,553. The average total outstanding liability per family has been worked out at Rs. 4092.

Outstanding position of Haveli block is estimated at Rs.2,06,159 at the same time outstanding interest is amounted to Rs.19,928. The total liability, therefore, comes to Rs.2,98,428. They have made repayments to the tune of Rs.92,269 which leaves the net outstanding liability of Rs.2,06,159. The average total outstanding per family has been worked out at Rs.4123.

Total borrowings of Rs.2,13,500 is the lowest in Mendhar block as compared to the other blocks of the division. It is lowest because of smaller magnitude of the advances taken by the agriculturists in this area. This area is treated as the most under developed area of the district Poonch. Outstanding in this area is worked out at Rs.1,56,404 and interest liability at Rs.37,785 whereas repayments are to the extent of Rs.94,881. This leaves a balance of Rs.1,56,404 as already pointed out earlier.

The table under reference further shows that the proportion of repayments to advances is as high as 39% in all the three blocks (R.S. Pura, Dansal and Mendhar); it is 33% in Haveli block. Similarly interest payable is 16% of the borrowings in all cases except Haveli Block where it is only 7%. It is lowest in Haveli block because the outstanding amount is lower as compared to other blocks. The rate of interest is, however, the same in all the blocks.

Per family outstanding liability is the highest in R.S. Pura block (Rs.14263), varies between Rs.3128 and Rs.9123 in other blocks.

It may be concluded that the outstandings possess a serious problem to the agriculturists operating in all the four blocks covered under survey. All these outstanding are in the form of bank borrowings and the interest thereon. The Govt. may come to the rescue by advising the banks to reschedule the repayment plan on a long-term basis so that the families are able to clear their debt liabilities without causing undue hardship due to the meagre resources of the agriculturists.

Table 4.26

Trend of Outstanding in Jammu Division on the Date of Survey

(In Rupees)

Block	Borrowings		Interest liability		Repayment		Outstanding		Average outstanding	
(Area covered under survey)	Total advance	%	Total interest	% of interest	Total repayments including subsidies	% of repayments	Total Outstanding	% of Outstanding	Outstanding per family	% of outstanding per ding family
1. R.S. Pura - Tehsil R.S. Pura, Distt. Jammu (Developed area of developed district)	9,27,035.00	100.00	1,52,257.33	16.42	3,65,933.00	39.47	7,13,359.33	76.95	14,267.00	76.95
2. Dansal - Tehsil Jammu, Distt. Jammu (under-developed area of developed district)	2,68,063.00	100.00	42,031.87	15.68	1,05,542.16	39.37	2,04,552.71	76.32	4,092.00	76.32
3. Haveli - Tehsil Poonch, Distt. Poonch (Developed area of under-developed district)	2,78,500.00	100.00	19,927.50	7.16	92,269.00	33.13	2,06,158.50	74.03	4,123.00	74.03
4. Mendhar - Tehsil Mendhar, Distt. Poonch (underdeveloped area of under developed district)	2,13,500	100.00	37,785.04	14.94	94,881.00	39.04	1,56,404.04	75.90	3,128.00	75.90
Total:	16,87,098.00	100.00	2,52,001.74	14.94	6,58,625.16	39.04	12,80,474.58	75.90	6,402.00	75.90

5
PROBLEMS OF AGRICULTURAL FINANCE

Agriculture is the backbone of our rural economy. To sustain, stimulate and strengthen its smooth functioning it requires perirhinal supply of agricultural credit with reasonability of interest.

Our study shows that a number of problems are coming in the way of effective and efficient operation of agricultural financing.

These problems based on the micro study, has been discussed under two broad heads:

1. Problems as faced by the agriculturists and
2. Problems identified by the financial institutions operating in the areas covered under survey.

PROBLEMS FACED BY THE AGRICULTURISTS

Problems faced by the agriculturists have been discussed as follows:

1. Defective Role of Surities and Guarantors

For acquiring loans, the farmers are required to furnish some security as well as surety to the bank. Security for loans may be provided by hypothecation of assets like tractors etc. owned by him, even this is not a simple proposition, every farmer does not have any other asset to offer except the land which he cannot offer. This becomes a big problem much in the way of obtaining finances from the bank. Many marginal farmers are unable to avail of this facility and their benefits and the benefits of agricultural development.

Similarly, for taking third party guarantee, bank generally insists on acquiring the guarantee of rich and influential persons. The borrower confronts a number of problems in relation to the guarantor. More often who is proposed to stand as a surety; secondly, he demands compensation for standing as surity. The agriculturists does not have money to pay him which causes lot of setback and embarrassment.

While verifying the loan case, the integrity of the borrower is ascertained from different angles. In this context, enquiry is made from the local persons, who wield influence in the village, like Sarpanch, rich farmers and other neighbourers of the borrower. The persons from whom enquiries are made, may or may not be on good terms with the proposed loanee. If they are on good terms with the loanee they conceal everything, which go against the borower and reveal everything which is in favour of borrower. On the other hand, if these persons are not on good terms with the proposed loanee, they would give wrong information regarding the person to the banker in order to create problems for the borrower.

2. Defective Role of Patwaries, Veterinary Doctors and Bank Officials

While processing the loan application and sanctioning the loan, the bank asks the borrower to submit the landholding records 'Jamabandi Records' i.e., latest holding of land by the borrower and other revenue records of the borrower. For acquiring these the borrower has to depend upon the patwaries and other officials of the revenue department. Proceedings through these officials are very slow and are not according to the actual facts. Each time the borrower has to obtain fresh certificate for getting loan sanctioned. The borrower is primarily dependent on the patwaries to get loans from the bank. If the patwari delays in issuing the land holding certificate, it will cause wastage of labour days of the borrower and non-availability of the timely credit from the bank. More often the patwaries play mischief to declare a big farmer as small or marginal farmer. Similarly they hesitate in issuing certificates according to the need of the farmers; if the farmers keep them happy, only then they could get the desired certificates.

Similarly, the verterinary doctors and the bank officials play their role when the borrower wants to buy the animals of his own choice. They make objections that health of animals is not good and not covered under the rules and procedure laid down for the purchase of such animals.

3. Insufficiency of Credit

It is seen that banks have not been able to assess the genuine needs of the borrowers, the borrowers are thus facing the problem of inadequacy of credit. Further loans are not granted as and when required to the borrowers apart from the problem of sufficient quantity of credit. If one who wants to purchase a horse-cart, only Rs.7,000 is given as loan or if he wants to get a pumpset for his field and only a sum of Rs.5,000 is given to him as loan, it will prove an exercise in futility as the amount is too meagre to carry on any worthwhile activity.

It is also found that some farmers have received loan for one purpose but due to insufficiency of the amount they have used it for other purposes or for even tempted to use it for domestic purposes.

Inadequacy of finance arises due to various factors: (i) improper estimates about the cultivators needs; (ii) arrears of past loans due to unforseen events like flood, drought, pestilenes, and other contingencies for fresh loans.

4. Problem of Cost and Profitability

Acquisition cost of credit in addition to interest is also a problem in financing agriculture. If the borrowers have to pay more as cost of credit it would certainly affect their capacity to avail credit. It may also discourage banking habits vis-a-vis banking activity. It is not necessary that they have to pay in cash the cost of credit, they may be paying in shape of loss of opportunity like wage earning days in visiting various offices for getting the loan sanctioned. For getting loan sanctioned, they have to visit revenue office, DRDA office, Co-operataive Society, Bank Office etc. The standard banking procedures are characterised by red-tape besides being complicated and irksome.

The components included in the cost of acquisition of loan are; cost of photographs, loss of wage earning days, revenue stamps, letter of guarantees, loan agreement, other unidentified charges being incurred at various stages to expedite the sanction of loans. The borrowers has also to pay insurance premium but it cannot be included in the acquisition cost of credit. It is not the cost but the borrower covers risk by insuring the unit. It is generally observed that demand for agricultural credit is more or less inelastic in relation to interest and other costs pertaining acquiring credit. Inspite of this fact, there is no denying the fact that the total cost of acquiring credit is quite depressing to the borrowers.

5. Problem of Using Borrowed Funds

Apart from the problems in obtaining the loans, borrowers have the problem of using their borrowed funds in an appropriate manner. Due to their illiteracy and ignorance, they face the problem of running their project/unit without technical knowledge which cause failure of project/unit and the borrower becomes defaulter unwillingly.

6. Terms and Conditions of Loan Taken are not Clear to the Farmers

Illiteracy and ignorance on the part of villagers are also the problem which exist in rural banking. Due to these reasons, they cannot understand banking rules, terms and conditions easily. Consequently majority of the farmers are not familiar with the significance and meaning of each of the credit schemes, interestingly enough, quite a few do not know even the interest rates of the loans which they availed. Some of the old farmers have a misconception that while they take loans from the bank, it goes on multiplying. Most of the farmers were found to be indifferent to taking loans because the terms and conditions are not clear to them. They do not know the rate of interest, subsidy and repayment conditions. It is more true in case of marginal, small and landless labourers.

7. Excessive Time in Borrowing

Seasonality of agricultural loans is another main problem. Crop loans are needed in the particular seasons, if the loans for crop are not advanced at the time of seasons, it will not serve the purpose for which they are taken. The loan disbursed after the season, will not be used for crop purposes. Even a delay for a week may require the agriculturist to wait for full year when that crop is to be repeated next year.

What is true of the crop loan is also true of the term loan which is taken for investment in fixed assets. For instance, if the term loan is released after the season of Rabi crop such as wheat, the investment will remain ideal practically for one year when wheat crop will be repeated next year. This will entail a high level of interst liability which the borrower shall have to incur without much benefit to him.

8. More Institututional Credit to Large Cultivators

Term loans has been an important component of agricultural finance. Out of the term loan the farmer may buy machine and equipments which may opt to agricultural productivity. Small and marginal farmers more often are not able to muster sufficient courage to going for such loans. They suffer in turn on account of their own deft. Conversely the large farmers get the facility from banks owing to their larger holdings and other influence with the financial institutions.

The study reveals that about 47% of the total loans goes to about 8.5% of the total population of large farmers remaining 43.25% of the loans shared by 73.5% of the total population of small and marginal farmers. This process has to be reversed so that the small and marginal farmers are benefitted by term loans.

9. Tight Repayment Schedules

Many times some of the small and marginal farmers are not able to get the benefit of crop loans owing to tight repayment schedules. A crop loan taken by the borrowers is expected to return it immediately after harvesting of the crop. He will be entitled to the crop loan for subsequent crop only when he has cleared off the earlier loan.

Sometimes, the pressure of repayment forces him to dispose of his produce at an unfavourable time which may fetch very low price from his farm produce. This causes lot of problem to him.

10. Mal-practices of DRDA Office

District Rural Development Agency (DRDA) is expected to sanction loan-cum-subsidy to the farmers. It recommend loan to the farmer of which a certain portion is the subsidy. For instance, if an agriculturist gets loan/subsidy amounting to Rs.2,000, it may be comprising of two components: (i) loan component which he is supposed to repay and (ii) the subsidy component which he is not supposed to repay to the govt. under various schemes attend for agricultural development.

Like most organisations of the Govt., DRDA is also a place where the corruption of different farms exists. The officials will not release the loan-cum-subsidy unless he greases the palm of the officials of this organisation. If he does not pay, his loan application may be delayed or even rejected on one excuse or the other. Under these circumstances he is forced to make payment to these officials so that his source of income flow does not dry up.

11. Defective Role of DRDA

DRDA is meant for assessing the viability of the project for which the loan-cum-subsidy is to be sanctioned in favour of the borrower. Unfortunately, it is not done. The need of the borrower is not properly appreciated, the officials are guided merely their vested interests rather than the need of the borrowers. For instance, if a borrower demands loan for the purchase of the cow, he is sanctioned for the purchase of a horse. This act affects the interests of the borrowers adversely.

PROBLEMS PERCEIVED BY THE INSTITUTIONS

An analysis of bank credit becomes incomplete if it is not followed by an appraisal of the difficulties by the Branch Managers, the operational instruments of the schemes. An attempt was, therefore, made in the course of the field investigation to obtain information on some operational problems of agricultural financing. The discussions with branch managers revealed that majority of the bank branches are facing the following problems:

1. Delay in Releasing the Subsidies by DRDA

District Rural Development Agency (DRDA) is such an agency which deals in sanctioning of subsidies to the borrowers under various Govt. schemes. Banks receive application for loan and subsidy from the borrowers through B.D.O. with his certificate regarding availability of amount for the purpose of subsidy. After verifying the loan case the banks forward the same to DRDA for the sanction of subsidy to the borrower. Generally, the officials of DRDA delay the loan case of the borrower owing to their vested interests. Under such circumstances, the bank can not sanction and disburse the amount unless it is intimated by the DRDA that the said borrower has been sanctioned the required amount of subsidy for the purchase of assets. This causes not only the problem for the bank to provide loan-cum-subsidy in time but also harrassment to the borrowers who keep on visiting the office of DRDA and banks.

2. Problem of Overdues

The discussions with Branch Managers revealed that majority of the branches are facing the recovery problems. If the repayment is not effected on the due date inclusive of limited grace period, the borrower becomes a defaulter and the amount outstanding becomes overdue. It is the major problem which is faced by the institutions.

The main causes of poor recovery of loans and overdues, as revealed by a number of branch managers are as follows:

(i) Every year either there is heavy rain or drought at one place or the other. Some natural calamities like floods, droughts etc., cause low productivity. They affect the repaying capacity of the loanees adversely. For instance, if the farmer takes crop loan and the crop is damaged due to heavy rain or drought, the borrower is unable to repay the amount. Again if the borrower has taken loan for the poultry farming and if the birds die due to some diseases, the borrower will not be able to repay the credit amount.

Apart from destroying the standing food crop, these calamities destroy the fodder crop also which leads to either non-availability or inadequate availability of fodder to the animals. This situation may either kill the animals or reduce their efficiency to work.

(ii) More often agriculturists divert their productive capital in the form of loans towards non-productive purposes such as social ceremonies. This results in reduction of income generation and in turn their capacity to repay.

(iii) Delay in disbursement of loans owing to fulfilment of formalities; releasing of subsidies by DRDA, which is a condition precedent to sanctioning of loans by banks etc., makes the utility of such financial support completely infractuous. When the crop season is over, the loan released by the bank will serve no purpose other than lying with the farmer. With the money lying idle with him, he may be tempted to divert it towards non-productive purposes.

(iv) Unforeseen expenses of the borrowers due to sickness, religious and social ceremonies, litigation and such other developments in the family also compels him to syphon off the borrowed money towards non-productive purposes and thus affect adversely his capacity to repay.

(v) More often the connivance between the agriculturists and the bank officials will lead to non-recovery of the loans. To fulfil the formalities, they will make peripheral attempt to recover the loans.

(vi) Most of the agriculturists have developed an attitude of wilful default because they feel the loan taken by them is Govt.'s money and the Govt.'s money is not meant to be repayed.

(vii) Sometimes, there is shortage of fertilizers, manures and pesticides at the time of cropping season. Non-availability of fertilisers and pesticides in a particular area creates problem both for the bank and the borrower. It will result in low production and the borrower has every reason to advocate that due to lower production he is unable to repay the loan taken by him.

(viii) Competition among financial institutions also induces the agriculturists to take loans from different banks for different purposes (e.g. fertilizers from co-operatives, short-term and medium-term from commercial banks and long-term loans from Land Development Co-operative Banks). Hence the instalments of all the loans taken for different purposes become due which results in difficulty for them to pay all the instalments almost at the same time. So they become the defaulters.

(ix) Rural poverty causes indebtness, low level incomes and the smallness of the farms, unemployment and disguised employment are the important contributed factors. It is this poverty which intend the farmers towards unproductive purposes. Consequently that keep on cummulative as he does not have the capacity to repay the loans. Whenever income is generated by him, is hardly sufficient to meet even his day to day expenditures on food, clothing and shelter.

(x) Politicisation of co-operatives does not allow the release of funds from such institutions in favour of weak uninfluencial farmers. They are not allowed to have any access to co-operative credit. Most of the funds are utilised by rich empowerful farmers who have a virtual monopoly on such credit. In the absence of agricultural credit, the farmer is unable to provide the needed inputs which leads to lower productivity and lower capacity to repay.

(xi) Absence of adequate follow-up measures to make recovery of loans. The loans accumulated as debts has also provide a lip to postpone repayments by the defaultering farmers. Efforts are to be made to activise the follow up machinery.

Factors identified above have created the recovery problem. Those who have the capacity to pay also do not like to repay because they have political links. The Branch Managers stated that whenever they take hard steps for recovery of loans, farmers go to their MLA and thus political pressure is applied to postpone recovery of loans.

3. Orgainsational Problems

Institutions providing finance are facing the organisational problems in the form of (i) overlapping of operational areas; (ii) double/ multiple financing, (iii) unhealthy competition among financial institutions etc.

While discussing with the branch managers, it has found that all these organisational problems are due to lack of co-ordination in between the various agencies working for rural development.

4. Procedural Problems

Majority of agricultural borrowers are illiterate. The documents which they have to execute appear to be cumbersome and time consuming, especially when timely financial assistance is a necessity. For instance to sanction long-term loan for well and pump-set, the procedure is that the borrower has to submit the certificates to be obtained from (i) co-operative society and all other banks operating in that area for 'no-dues', (ii) Ground water Services and Development Agency for ground-water availability, (iii) electricity department for power connection, etc. Loan procedures are internal problems of commercial banks and have to be solved through their initiative and inventiveness.

5. Political Problems

Politics in our country is based on caste, creed, language and religions, this creates rivalry among various factions right from the national to the panchayat level. Even the banking institutions in rural areas are pressurised to give loans or extend moratorlum facilities to a particular group of farmers. In small villages ridden with political and communal factionalism, commercial bank personnel is bound to come under undesirable pressure. Such political pressure force the institutions to sacrifice the norms of sound creditability to the farmers.

6. Absence of Proper Institutional Agency to Control Misdirection of Financial Assistance by the Agriculturists

There is no institutional arrangement to ensure that the agriculturists does not divert funds from one project scheme to another. More often this practice misfires with the result that the borrower looses a sizeable portion of the assistance received from the institutions. When the project becomes unsuccessful, capacity to pay of the borrowers will reduce. Under these circumstances there is need for proper control on misdirection of funds, so that he could maintain his capacity to pay. This put the problem to the financial institutions to get back the support extended to the agriculturists.

7. Inadequacy of Staff

Some of the branch managers complained that in the matter of implementing their agricultural credit schemes, they were handicapped by non-availability of adequate and competent staff, particularly field staff at their branches.

Because of low volume of agricultural advances at some of the rural branches, it was obviously uneconomic to appoint field staff which is crucially needed to supervise agricultural credit schemes. Sometimes it is difficult to recruit field officers and assistances from the regions where they are required. Often the staff lack the right attitude towards providing agricultural advances because of the conventional inspection and other procedures.

The problem of small branches may be solved by pooling the operational area with other bigger branches and bearing the proportionate cost which may be much lower as compared to carrying independent activities.

8. Waiving of Loans upto Rs.10,000 - Govt.'s Policy

The policy of Janta Govt. to waive of loans upto Rs.10,000 taken by agriculturists has given wrong signals. The agriculturists have developed the feeling that they may continue to receive the loans without paying to the financial institutions which may be ultimately waived off through Govt. policy. This thinking encouraged in the minds of the agriculturists, has adversely affected the recovery position of the banks. Inspite of the follow up measures taken up by the banks the agriculturists keeps on postponing payment on one protext to the other, but the root cause of such delay practices on the part of the agriculturists was the wrong decision taken by the Govt. This wrong decision go on a political decision to catch votes in the election has been instrumental in an entwine the very fabric of sound banking principles and policies.

9. Finance Discipline

Every financial institution dealing in agricultural finance is required to maintain finance discipline to avail refinance facilities from the NABARD, this refinance is available subject to the condition that 30% of the previous loans has been refunded to NABARD. When the agriculturists do not repay the loans, it becomes problem for the banks to fulfil this commitment to NABARD.

10. Lack of Efficient Management

Most of the bank managers are without professional experience to enforce the appropriate tools and techniques of management to improve the level of efficiency in their respective organisations. Their training programme, whatever may be lacked gravely the input of management and administration.

Thus alternative are suggested to achieve this objective: (i) their training may be restrained with appropriate input of administration and management; (ii) the officers may be exposed to the latest tools and techniques of managing people and organisations in the management development programmes specially designed and structured for them.

The foregoing discussion shows that two set of problems are faced in the process of disbursement of finances to agriculturists. One of them pertains to the agriculturists and the other to the institutions. The problems of agriculturists relate to the surities and guarantors, insufficiency of credit available to them, problem of cost, and terms and conditions on which finance are provided to them. The purpose of the finances, gets forefeited if it is not received by the agriculturists at the right time. Similarly needy agriculturists have to face lot of problems because of their feeble influence with the financing agencies.

For this purpose efforts should be made to stimulate the procedure regarding sanctioning and disbursement of financial assistance in such a manner that delays and nepatism and other extraneous considerations are reduced to the minimum.

The problems faced by the financial institutions which are of procedural and organisational nature have to be removed to make the entire programme result-oriented. The procedure should be simplified so that delays and asidable formalities could be avoided to the benefit of the poor and marginal farmers on the one hand and the banking organisation on the other. Simultaneously, efforts have also to be made to avoid duplication or overlapping of finances for a single project by establishing a liaison with other financial organisations/institutions. For this purpose, there is the need for proper co-ordination which may be forced by organising periodic meetings of all the heads of financial institutions operating in that area where such cases could be detected. The success of this co-ordination efforts depends on the will and commitment of the officials of financial institutions to achieve the above said objective.

6
CONCLUSION AND SUGGESTIONS

The purpose of this study was to identify the sources of agricultural finance, role of institutional agencies in providing finance for agricultural operations, problems faced by the agriculturists and the institutions, and suitable measures to overcome these problems. The data was collected from a sample of 200 beneficiaries belonging to twenty villages spreading over four blocks of Jammu Division. Of the four blocks one each belongs to the developed area and other to under-developed area of Jammu and Poonch Districts. In the selected villages various bank branches were also contacted for study purposes.

On the basis of analysis and investigation, following conclusions have been drawn:

Total holdings in the state in 1985-86 was 11,84,584 hectares with an average holding of 0.86 hectares per farmer. The land put to non-agricultural uses also recorded an increase in 1985-86. In the land use pattern in 1985-86, 70.57 per cent of the total operational area was reported as net area sown. Irrigated area formed 41.35% of the gross cultivated area. During 1985-86 about 34.19 thousand tonnes of chemical fertilizers were distributed among the farmers. Inspite of this fact, agricultural productivity continued to be lower. The Govt. has to secure foodgrains from the centre to meet people's requirements of foodgrains.

Agriculture is the most important component of the state's

economy. It contributes more than 40% to the total income of the state. About 2/3 of the total population depends directly or indirectly on this sector.

The Govt. has paid the needed attempt for its growth and development by way of providing fertilizers at subsidised rates and other inputs like seed etc. to increase agricultural productivity.

Inspite of these facts, agriculture in the state has not succeeded in making proper headway. Production of foodgrains has remained stationery for the last many years.

There is, therefore, the need for improving the state of agriculture in such a manner that productivity increases so that income and in turn savings and capital form go to contribute effectively to the process of growth and development. With the increase in productivity, its capacity to absorb more people within its fold increases which will reduce the incidence of unemployment, under employment and even disguised unemployment.

The basic component, apart from other elements for augmenting agricultural production is the credit requirement of the farmers. The vast majority of the farmers have no savings for investment and for inputs; they have to depend on borrowings. If finance is not available to them, they will not be able to perform agricultural operations.

The credit needs of the farmers can be classified under three heads: (i) short-term; (ii) medium-term; and (iii) long-term. The agencies which provide such finances are: Commercial Banks, Regional Rural Banks, Co-operative Societies and Land Development Co-operative Banks.

Outstanding advances to agriculture in the state during 1986 was estimated at Rs.50,00,17,000 which has gradually increased to Rs.87,78,62,000 during 1989.

Beneficiaries are identified for financial support on the basis of the following parameters:

(i) Distribution of population by sex and age,

(ii) Average family size,

(iii) Educational status,

(iv) Size and type of holdings,

(v) Extent of Tenancy,

(vi) Economic Status,

(vii) Farm family assets and

(viii) Family incomes

The survey conducted by the researcher has revealed that holding size of a farmer is too small; it is estimated at 3.43 acres on an average; incidentally about 51.60% of land is irrigated. Out of 1283 persons covered under survey about 25% are in the age group of earners and the remaining 75% are dependents. Per capita land in Jammu division is 0.50 acre. The annual average family income of the borrower has been estimated at Rs.11,136 which comes to an average of per capita income of Rs.1736 per annum. Out of the total sample of 200 beneficiaries, 69.5% are illiterate. Out of the total population (1283 persons) covered under survey about 319 persons are educated upto primary, middle, matric and graduate levels. The study reveals that the educated farmers have obtained larger volume of credit as compared to illiterate farmers. Land is the major asset of all the farmers covered under survey. It has accounted for 80% of the total value of assets of the farmers.

The survey disclosed that a farmer on an average has received credit to the tune of Rs.3970 from commercial banks, Rs.1382 from the regional rural banks, Rs.2459 from co-operative land development banks and Rs.625 from co-operative banks and societies. In this way all these financial agencies have provided total financial support of Rs.16,87,098 as loan to the two hundred families covered under survey. Out of this sum, 47.06% has been supplied by the commercial banks. The proportion of the Central Co-operative Land Development Bank has been worked out at 29.15%. The Regional Rural Banks have provided loans to the tune of 16.38% and the Co-operative Banks and Societies 7.41%. This shows that commercial banks are the most important agency to provide agricultural finance.

Survey reveals that out of the total distributed finance by all financial institutions in Jammu Division, maximum proportion of 49.13% is received by the large farmers. Other categories of beneficiaries in order of importance are marginal farmers (41.41%), small farmers (4.57%), landless labourers (3.13%) and medium farmers (1.76%).

Agricultural finance is generally required for the purchase of inputs, machinery and implements, live stock and for improvement in farm building etc. The study reveals that the machinery and implements account for the maximum proportion of borrowing to the tune of 49.93%. Other purposes in order of importance are live stock (35.85%), inputs (8.16%) and farm building improvement (6.06%).

The financial assistance obtained by the marginal farmers and landless labourers has largely been devoted to the purchase of live stock; this constitutes more than 73% and 92% of their respective total borrowings. The relative importance of borrowings for farm building, improvement and investment is higher among small cultivators (42.01%). The proportionate borrowing for inputs is higher among medium farmers (41.08%). Conversely, large farmers have reported a higher proportion of borrowing (93.17%) for machinery and implements.

Among the financial agencies, commercial banks and Regional Rural Banks are the major sources of finance for multipurposes but the Co-operative Societies have generally specialised in financing inputs.

The data provided by the field study indicate that outstanding liabilities of the beneficiaries have exceeded the repayment by about 66%. The total outstanding advances of all the two hundred families on the date of survey has been estimated at Rs.16,87,098. The liability of outstanding interest has been worked at Rs.2,52,002 approximately. Total repayments on the date of survey has been reported at Rs.6,58,625. This leaves a balance of Rs.12,80,474. The average total outstanding liability (principal and interest) per family has been estimated at Rs.6402. The proportion of outstanding interest to advances is as high as 15%. Similarly, all the two hundred families on an average have been able to clear their outstanding liabilities to the extent of 33%.

Though the repayment pattern suggests that landless labourers in general are more conscious of repayments as they have cleared their outstanding liabilities to the tune of 52.43%.

There are certain problems which are faced by both the agriculturists as well as by the institutions which cause hinderance in the smooth functioning of the system of agricultural finance.

The micro study further reveals that the problems of the agriculturists relate to the surities and guarantors, insufficiency of credit, problem of cost and profitability, problem of using funds, ignorance as to the terms and conditions of loan taken, non-availability of credit in time, more credit to large cultivators, tight repayment schedules, corrupt practices of DRDA office and defective role of DRDA in granting subsidies.

The problems, view point of the institution relates to delay in releasing subsidies by the District Rural Development Agency (DRDA) which further causes delay in disbursement of loans to the agriculturists, banks do not entertain loan applications unless subsidy has been sanctioned by DRDA in favour of the beneficiaries, other problems pertain to recovery of loans and overdues, problem of recovery and overdues arise because of natural calamities, delay in disbursement of loans, unforeseen expenditure of the borrowers owing to illness, marriage or other social ceremonies or even litigation, wilful default on the part of certain agriculturists, inconnivance with agriculturists, or political influence. More often the capacity to pay of the farmers gets adversely affected owing to lower productivity of their land; the productivity may be lower, apart from other factors, on account of shortage in the supply of fertilizers, pesticides at cropping season and improper coordination between financial institutions and rural development agencies/departments.

Besides the problems of recovery and overdues, institutions are facing the organisational problems, procedural problems, staff problems and the problem of political interference. These problems have further been compounded by the absence of institutional agency to provide control over misdirection of productive finance towards non-productive purposes.

All these problems enumerated above have exercised an adverse effect over financing of agricultural operations in Jammu Division. The efforts made by the Govt. have partially successed in streamlining the situation.

Suggestions

On the basis of the analysis and investigation made, following suggestions are offered to overcome the problems faced by the agriculturists and the institutions:

1. One of the biggest problems, which the poor cultivators are facing in obtaining agricultural finances from institutions is the problem of surities and guarantors. The financial institutions accept guarantee of well to do farmers, big landlords, surpanches and other party functionary of the villages. In fact, these people have least interest in poor cultivators and hesitate to stand as a surity for poor cultivators unless he promised to compensate them properly. To overcome the problem of guarantor/surity, it is suggested that (i) the persons referred to above who are not prepared to stand as guarantor/surities for the poor farmers may be replaced by other villagers who though commanding social respect may not be monetarily very sound like village teacher, master craftsman or even some punches; (ii) the system of group guarantee may introduced. Persons comprising group may have economic creditability on the one hand and social status on the other.

2. To mitigate the hardship to the farmers in obtaining land holding records each time from the Patwaries and other officials of the Revenue Department. It is suggested that the State Government should issue Pass-Books to the owners and tenants as prima facie evidence to the rights in land of an agriculturists.

3. Exploitation of borrowers by veterinary doctors and bank officials in purchase of live stock be stopped. A voucher system be introduced and the Govt. should make such an arrangement that the borrowers can purchase the needed live stock against the voucher through Govt.'s Intensive Cattle Development Centres approved from time to time by the State Govt. in consultation with the banks.

4. Lending policies of the bank should be brought in confirmity with the requirements of the borrowers. The loans should be need based and the needs should be assessed on the basis

of actual requirement of the land and other agricultural operations. When a loan is not commensurate to the needs and is insufficient than the purpose of loan is forefeited. It is, therefore, suggested that fixation of amount of loan for different jobs must be avoided. Loans should be need based rather than norm based.

5. The acquisition cost of credit is quite high. It has been observed that the borrowers do not care much for this aspect when they are in need of loans, with the result the cost of credit continues to very high which he comes to know when he is required to start the repayment process. This makes agricultural credit inelastic in relation to cost of acquisition. It is suggested that this cost can be broken into avoidable and unavoidable costs. The avoidable cost can completely be eliminated while the unavoidable can be minimised. The avoidable may be the cost of hypothecating the assets, identified charges etc. Hypothecation can be done on loan agreement on judicial paper. The unavoidable cost which can be minimised are costs due to loss of wage earning days, incidental experiences etc. A resemblance between these costs may be established as far as possible.

6. Problem of proper use of funds can also be removed by guiding the farmers. There should be some agency in the village which could provide necessary guidance to farmers as to the proper use of funds. In the beginning, an additional post in the banks can be created to do this work. Banks can make adequate arrangements to enable beneficiaries to deal with unexpected problems that may arise in project implementation. Later on Banks through their technical, promotional and supervisory services can assist farmers to ensure that there is no diversion of funds from productivity to non-productive sectors.

7. Ignorance regarding rules and regulation due to illiteracy of the farmers is also one of the serious problem in rural banking. It is suggested that banks should render advice to the farmers regarding different rules, terms and conditions etc. for the loan and other facilities. They should be advised very sympathetically, the educated persons of the villages,

the local influential persons, the surpanches, gramsevaks etc. should take the illiterate farmers into their confidence and should educate them regarding rules, terms and conditions of the bank loans. These farmers may also be covered under adult literacy programme.

8. Adequate and timely loans alone can help the farmers. The procedures for loan must be simplified and short-circuited keeping in view the seasonality of agriculture. Since agriculture is a seasonal industry even a delay of a week might mean a delay of one year.

9. It should be freely admitted that commercial banks favour the large against the small and rich against the poor. Efforts should be made to reverse the process. Banks should ensure that the needs of small cultivators are adequately met on a priority basis. Commercial banks should, therefore, have to address themselves and their procedures in such a manner as to provide a smooth and increasing flow of credit to marginal and small farmers.

10. The problem of disposing of the produce by the borrowers at an unfavourable time under pressure of repayments, can be set aside if the repayment schedule has sufficient time span to dispose of the crops. The other alternative may be that in such needy cases a provision of rescheduling of payment plan may be implemented so that the agriculturists could have sufficient breeding time.

11. Another problem which is faced by the agriculturists and the institutions is delay in sanctioning of subsidies by the DRDA (District Rural Development Agency) officials for their vested interests. The malpractices of DRDA officials can be minimised if the Govt. could take some harsh steps against the corrupt official of DRDA. It is suggested that the functioning of DRDA may be restructured by the elements of training, supervision and control. In addition the officials involved in such malpractices may be given exemplary punishment.

12. While loans to agriculturists are necessary for boosting up agricultural productions, their timely repayment with inter-

est is also equally necessary for rebuilding the bank's capacity to give further loans. It is, therefore, suggested that there should be a proper plan for repayment on the basis of income earning capacity rather than making borrowers to pay in equal instalments over a span of time. This suggestion has been made even in the light of the differential rates of interest payable by the poor and marginal farmers. Many such farmers sometime do not have the capacity to pay even to pay the principal and thc interest charges.

While doing so, the administration has to ensure that the agriculturists do not allow deliberately to accumulate their liability to desire political liverage as was done unpredicіously by the Janata Dal Government.

Moreover, from time to time, "Recovery Weeks" should be organised with full programme of recovery by the rural banking institutions. Majority of the managers opine that the recovery problem can reasonably be reduced if the branch managers are vested with the power of both lending and recovery, rather than following the present policy of keeping the powers with the head office. As it stands today, a branch manager has to seek the advice of his head office on the type of action to be taken against a defaulting account.

13. In case of genuine difficulty arising from unforeseen calamities such as crop-failures, sickness or death in the family, sickness or death of bullocks etc., a grace period for repayment should be granted or short-term loan should be converted into medium term loan. RBI and NABARD should issue the necessary guidelines to banks and co-operatives in regard to the extent of relief to be provided in each case. However, it will be necessary for credit institutions to build up adequate field staff to access genuine cases of hardships.
14. The credit should be "Supervised Credit". The main reason for misutilisation was found to be inadequate post-lending supervision which was due to lack of staff, lack of communication and conveyance facilities etc. All these difficulties and gaps may be overcome by taking suitable steps. For supervised credit a bank needs adequate supervisory staff.

Bankers through their technical, promotional and supervisory activities will have to make sure that farms, in fact, become going concerns. There should be adequate post-disbursal supervision of the end-use of credit. Banks should be able to provide their borrowers guidance to deal with unexpected difficulties that may arise in project implementation. Through these support mechanisms, banks can prevent many honest borrowers from joining the rank of defaulters.

15. Banks are entitled to the fullest possible support of the state machinery to effect recoveries from wilful defaulters. In case of willful defaults additional penal measures should be imposed, including attachment of property. The recovery proceedings should be initiated at the time of the next harvest. The purchaser of produce with prior arrangements can deduct a portion of the bank's loan from the sale proceeds.

16. In the interest of timely recovery of their loans, banks have to be aware of all linkage and should prevail upon the local development administration for timely provision of essential inputs, infrastructure and marketing support needed for successful implementation of agricultural projects.

17. The agricultural department should also see that there is no shortage of fertilisers and pesticides during the period when they are needed. Advances by the bank will be of no use if the raw materials for agriculture are not available in required quantum and at proper time.

18. Most of the farmers in the villages are incapable of running poultry, piggery and dairy farming on scientific lines. The loans for these farms particularly for poultry should be advanced only to those who have sufficient experience and knowledge. The farmers should take instructions to run the farms on scientific lines.

19. There should be proper co-ordination of the lending operations of different institutional credit agencies namely, commercial bank branches, co-operative credit societies, Regional Rural Banks and so on with a view to minimising the danger of multiple financing resulting in financial indisci-

pline. This can be solved to a reasonable extent by resorting to the following means:

(i) Each financial unit should be assigned a certain group of villages according to the convenience and it should be given the primary responsibility of meeting all priority sector credit needs of the specified areas.

(ii) Introduction of identity cards for cultivators. This card should contain all land holding details of the cultivator, his credit transaction such as purposes, security, etc. and details of the farm production. It should be insisted at the time of sanction of every loan whenever a financial institution makes an advance, it should affix its seal to denote the sanction of a credit facility, which should be cancelled under authentication by the agency under seal when the facility is cleared.

20. Poor recovery position of the institutions due to rural poverty can be solved if efforts are made to increase the income of the borrowers on the one hand and ensure the remunerative prices for their output on the other.

21. The complicated and cumbersome procedures of the bank in the agricultural lending should be properly streamlined so as to give adequate and timely credit to the farmers. NABARD and RBI should bring out in a booklet from its simplified procedures to be followed by the credit institution at grass root levels in the disbursement of short, medium and long term loans, terms and conditions of such loans and relief/ concessions available etc. The booklet should be in simple language so that both bank staff and intending beneficiaries may get acquainted with the rules and procedures. Similarly paper work connected with securing loans should be reduced to the minimum.

In conclusion, it can be stated that the success of the agricultural financing in Jammu Division depends upon simple and prompt loaning procedure, progressive policies ensuring substantial service to small farmers, facilitating people's participation, scientific outlook in technical matters, efficient management and effective control and supervision over the utilisation of the loans.

At last but not the least, it is suggested that loans should be objective oriented. Attention should be given to the development rather fulfilling the unnecessary formalities for availing loans. If the Govt. wants to solve the problem of agricultural financing, it must establish a separate cell for helping the borrowers in managing and using their funds. The only formality should be that an unauthorised agriculturist does not manage to receive the loan benefits. Loans should by and large be granted considering the earning capacity of the project for which the loan is to be sought. The lending institutions ought to adopt a liberal attitude towards accommodating the legitimate needs of farmers more specially of poor and marginal farmers.

If the suggestions mentioned above are implemented, they will go a long way in improving the financing position of agriculturists covered under study in particular and other agriculturists in general.

APPENDICES

QUESTIONNAIRE

Area : Developed/Under-Developed

1. Identification

(i) Province ____________ (ii) Distt.. ____________

(iii) Tehsil ____________ (iv) Village ____________

(v) Block ____________ (vi) Date of Interview ____________

(vii) Name of the Head of Family ____________

(viii) Respondent ____________ (ix) Religion ____________

2. Household Composition

S.No.	*Name*	*Relation-ship with the res-pondent*	*Sex*	*Age*	*Age at the time of marriage*	*Eco. Status E D*	*Edu-cation*
1.							
2.							
3.							
4.							
5.							
6.							
7.							
8.							
9.							
10.							

3. Occupational Structure

S. No.	*Name of the working member/ members of the family*	*Sex*	*Nature of Employment*				*Total Income*	*Unem-ployed if any*
			Agr	*Ind*	*Service*	*Others*		
1.								
2.								
3.								
4.								
5.								
6.								
7.								
8.								

4. Household Characteristics

Size of land	*Cultivated*		*Uncultivated*	
	Irrigated	*Unirrigated*	*Irrigated*	*Unirrigated*
(i) Land owned				
(ii) Land leased out				
(iii) Land leased in				
(iv) Total land available for production				

5. Other Holdings

Particulars	*In working condition*	*Not in working condition*	*Total value*
(i) Machinery & Implements			
(a) Tractor			
(b) Thresher			
(c) Trailer & Trollies			
(d) Seed-cum-fertilizer drill			
(e) Sheller			
(f) Ploughs (iron) & Harrows			
(g) Ploughs (wooden)			
(h) Oil Engines & Electric Motor			
(i) Bullock Carts			
(j) Cane crusher			
(k) Ridger			
(l) Process Equipment			
(m) Others			
(n) Spraying pump			
(o) Electric Chaffcutter			
(p) Store Bins			
(q) Poultry Equipments			
(r) Dairy Equipments			
(s) Others			
(ii) Live Stock			
(a) Bullocks			
(b) Cows			
(c) He-buffaloes			
(d) She-buffaloes			

(e) Camels

(f) Donkeys

(g) Goats

(h) Sheeps

(i) Pigs

(j) Poultry Birds

(k) Others

(i)

(ii)

(iii)

---

6. Income From Farm Produce

Crops	*Total Produce*	*Self Consumption*	*Marketable surplus*	*Market Price*	*Income*
Rabi					
Kharif					

7. Income From Other Sources

	Price	Amount
(i) Sale of livestock		
(ii) Sale of milk and milk products		
(iii) Sale of poultry products		
(iv) Income from hiring out of farm equipment		
(a) Tractor		
(b) Other equipments		
(1)		
(2)		
(3)		
(4)		

(v) Non-farm Income
   (a) Income from Transport
   (b) Income from household industries
   (c) Services
   (d) Others
      (i)
      (ii)
      (iii)

8. Structure of Financial Agencies in Financing Agriculture

(I) Have you borrowed money for financing your agriculture? If yes then specify the source of borrowings.

Sources	*Total amount borrowed*	*Last year's balance*	*Interest paid*		*Total amount repaid*	*Balance during the year*
			Total	*Last year*		
(a) S.F.C. etc. and other term lending institutions						
(b) Govt.						
(c) Regional Rural Bank						
(d) Land Development Bank						
(e) Public Sector Banks other than R.R.B. Name & Address:						

(f) Other Commercial Banks Name & Address:	
(g) Co-operative Banks	
(h) Moneylenders	
(i) Friends & Relatives	
(j) Co-operative Societies	
(k) Others	
Total	

9. Purpose of Borrowings

(I) Have you borrowed for input purposes, if yes specify:

	Amount	
	Total	Last Year
(a) Seeds		
(b) Manure		
(c) Fertilizers		
(d) Pesticides		
(e) Irrigation charges		
(f) Others:		
(i)		
(ii)		
(iii)		

(II) Have you borrowed for purchase of machinery and implements? If yes, how much and specify the items:

	Amount borrowed			
	Year	Value	Total	Last Year
(a) Tractor				
(b) Thresher				
(c) Trailer				
(d) Trollies				
(e) Seed-cum-fertilizer drill				
(f) Sheller				
(g) Ploughs (wooden)				
(h) Ploughs (Iron) & Harrows				
(i) Oil Engines & Electric Motors				
(j) Bullock Carts				
(k) Cane Crusher				
(l) Ridger				
(m) Process Equipment				
(n) Spraying Pump				
(o) Electric Chaffcutter				
(p) Store Bins				
(q) Others:				
(i)				
(ii)				
(iii)				

(III) Have you borrowed for farm building, improvement and investment? if yes, specify the items:

	Amount borrowed			
	Year	Value	Total	Last Year
(a) Purchase of land				
(b) Reclamation and improvement of land				
(c) Construction of Khuls				
(d) Tubewell/Pumping set				
(e) Purchase of indigenous minor implements				
(f) Purchase of improved implements				
(g) Huts				
(h) Cattle Sheds				
(i) Bunding & levelling				
(j) Orchards & Plantation				
(k) Others				

(IV) Have you borrowed for live stock? If yes, specify the items:

	Amount borrowed			
	Year	Value	Total	Last Year
(a) For cultivation and draft:				
1. Bullocks				
2. Cows				
3. He-buffaloes				
4. She-buffaloes				
5. Camels				

(b) Dairy Stock

1. Cows in milk
2. Cows not in milk
3. Buffaloes in milk
4. Buffaloes not in milk

(c) Other for draft & riding

1. Donkeys
2. Goats
3. Sheep
4. Pigs

10. Security Offered for Loan Borrowed:

Have you offered security for borrowing loan? If yes, specify:

	Value	Loan taken on security Total	Last Year
(a) Land			
(b) Building			
(c) Crops			
(d) Any other asset			
(e) Guarantee if any			

Abbreviations:

E. Earner, D. Dependent, M. Mail, Mn. Main, F. Female, S. Subsidy

Remarks:

QUESTIONNAIRE : APPLICABLE TO THE BANK OPERATING IN THE CONCERNED AREA.

Area : Developed/Under-Developed

1. Identification:

(i) Province ________________ (ii) Distt.. ________________

(iii) Tehsil ________________ (iv) Village ________________

(v) Block ________________ (vi) Date of Interview ____________

(vii) Name of the Bank ________________________________

(viii) Name & Designation of Respondent ________________

2. Particulars of Advances

Have you advanced the finances for agricultural purposes? If yes, then give the following details:

S. No.	*Name and address of the desired borrowers*	*Name of the project*	*Total amount advanced*	*Period of loan*	*Rate of interest*	*Period of instalment*
1	2	3	4	5	6	7
1.						
2.						
3.						
4.						
5.						
6.						
7.						
8.						
9.						
10.						

S. No.	*Amount of instalment including interest*	*Amount of Interest*	*Total amount refunded*	*Balance*	*Security/Surety held*
	8	9	10	11	12
1.					
2.					
3.					
4.					
5.					
6.					
7.					
8.					
9.					
10.					

3. General Information

(a) How do you assess the profitability and suitability of the Project?

____

____

____

____

____

(b) Do loanees pay instalment in time? ______________________________

(c) What measures you take in case of defaulters?

____

____

(d) Do you give second loan if the loanees need for the same project?

____

(e) Are you given loan not in cash in case of live stock? If yes, why?

____

(f) What are the causes of delay in sanctioning the loans?

(i)______________________________

(ii)______________________________

(iii)______________________________

(iv)______________________________

(v)______________________________

(g) How much time you take in sanctioning the loan?

____

(h) How many times an applicant has to visit the Branch for getting loans?

____

4. Problems in Agricultural Finances

(a)______________________________

(b)______________________________

(c)______________________________

(d)______________________________

(e)______________________________

(f)______________________________

(g)______________________________

(h)______________________________

12. Report on Development Banking in India, 1979-80, issued by Industrial Development Bank of India.
13. *Financing of Agriculture by Commercial Banks* — Report of a Seminar on Dec. 6 to 8, 1968 RBI.
14. *The Indian Journal of Commerce* (A quarterly of the Indian Commerce Association).
15. B.M. Choubey: *Institutional Finance for Agricultural Development.*
16. P.K. Benerjee: *Indian Agricultural Economy.*
17. S.S.M. Desai: *Rural Banking in India.*
18. O.P. Goyal: *Financial Institutions and Economic Growth of India.*
19. N.S. Gupta & Amerjit Singh: *Agricultural Development of States in India.*
20. John W. Melior: *The Economics of Agricultural Development.*
21. P.V. Shenoi: *Agricultural Development in India - A New Strategy in Management.*
22. S.S. Johl, T.R. Kapur: *Farm Business Management.*
23. Theodore N. Beekman: *Credit and Collections Management & Theory.*
24. A.P. Mehta & O.P. Bhardwaj: *Money Banking and International Trade.*
25. Rudder Dutt & K.P.M. Sundharm: *Indian Economy.*
26. C.B. Mamoria: *Agricultural Problems of India.*
27. V.G. Rao Prakash Malya: *Agricultural Finance by Commercial Banks.*
28. B.M. Desai & Y. Narayana Rao: *Project Approach in Agricultural Financing.*
29. Kumar Kant Jha: *Agricultural Finance in Nepal.*
30. Mahfoozur Rehman: *Co-operative Credit and Agricultural Development.*
31. Misra, Puri: *Indian Economy.*

32. Nand Kishore Jha: *Bank Finance and Green Revolution in India.*

33. Charanjit Chanana: *Agricultural Finance in India - Role of Commercial Banks.*

34. Rajendra Gupta: *Agricultural Finance : A Long Term Problem.*

35. V.S. Mahajan: *Studies in Indian Banking and Finance.*

36. Rama Nand Pandey: *Commercial Banks and Rural Development.*

37. Dr. Tandon & Dr. Dhandyal: *Principles and Methods of Farm Management.*

38. Basul J. Moore: *An Introduction to the Theory of Finance.*

39. Carl A. Danten Merlet T. Welshans: *Principles of Finance.*

40. Sadhu and Singh: *Impact of New Agricultural Strategy.*

41. S.M. Ghosal: *Agricultural Financing in India.*

42. L.C. Jain: *Indigenous Banking in India.*

43. A.M. Khusro: *Reading in Agricultural Economics.*

44. C.H. Shah: *Problems of Small Farmers.*

45. S.S. Jogl and C.V. Moore: *Farm Financial Management.*